Quick Reference Guide™

Corel® WordPerfect® Suite 8 Professional

Diana Rain

DDC Publishing

275 Madison Ave., NY 10016
http://www.ddcpub.com

DDC Publishing, Inc.
275 Madison Avenue
New York, New York 10016
Phone: 800-528-3897
Fax: 800-528-3862
http://www.ddcpub.com

First DDC Publishing, Inc. Printing
10   9   8   7   6   5   4   3

Catalog No. G32

ISBN: 1-56243-543-4

Printed in the United States of America

INTRODUCTION

The *DDC Quick Reference Guide for Corel WordPerfect Suite 8 Professional* saves you time searching through technical manuals for directions. Step-by-step instructions for essential procedures using mouse and keyboard techniques help you get answers fast.

Corel WordPerfect Suite 8 Professional provides you with an integrated set of tools for producing results quickly. Word processor, spreadsheet, database , and presentation programs work together to help you complete your work faster than ever before. Use Corel Experts (available on the Help menu) to guide you through tasks such as creating databases and exporting data.

This guide is designed to provide essential commands for the Corel WordPerfect Suite 8 programs, concentrating on commonly used features.

Diana Rain

Author:	*Diana Rain*
Managing Editor:	*Kathy Berkemeyer*
English/Technical Editor:	*Rebecca J. Fiala*
Layout:	*Julia Ingram*

WORDPERFECT 8

Index

iv   Index

QUATTRO PRO

PARADOX

PRESENTATIONS

INDEX

WordPerfect

ADDRESS BOOK

Stores addresses, phone numbers, and other information that you can use to insert in documents, automatically dial phone numbers, and create mailing labels and envelopes. You can create additional address books.

Open Address Book

Click **T**ools, **A**ddress Book..................... `Alt`+`T`, `A`

Add Address

—IN ADDRESS BOOK—

1. Click tab corresponding .... `Ctrl`+`Tab`
   to address book to open.

   > NOTE: Each tab in the **Corel Address Book** dialog
   > box represents a different address book.

2. Click `Add...` .... `Alt`+`A`

3. **Select entry type** (**Person**,................. `↑` `↓`, `↵`
   Organization, or **Resource**).

4. Fill in desired information for new entry.

5. Click `OK` .... `↵`
   to finish adding entry.

   OR

   a. Click `New` .... `Alt`+`W`
      to create another entry.

   b. Click `Yes` .... `↵`
      to save changes.

      OR

      Click `No` .... `Alt`+`N`
      to delete entry.

   c. Repeat steps 4 and 5 as necessary.

Close Address Book Dialog Box

Click [Close]

Edit Address

—IN ADDRESS BOOK—

1. Click desired address book tab .... `Ctrl` + `Tab`

2. Select address to edit .... `↑` `↓`

3. Click [Edit...] .... `Alt` + `I`

4. Edit information as desired.

5. Click [OK] to finish editing .... `↵`

Format Address

The format determines the address entry information to include when you follow the **Insert Address into Document** *procedure. For example, the U.S. Standard format inserts the name, address, city, state, and zip code whereas the U.S. Standard with Country format includes all of the above information as well as the country.*

—IN ADDRESS BOOK—

1. Click desired address book tab .... `Ctrl` + `Tab`

2. Select address to format .... `↓` `↑`

3. Click [Format...] .... `Alt` + `F`

4. Select desired **Format** .... `↑` `↓`

Example of format is shown to the right of the **Format** *list.*

5. Click [OK] .... `↵`

WordPerfect

Insert Address into Document

—IN ADDRESS BOOK—

1. Click desired address book tab .... `Ctrl`+`Tab`
2. Select address to insert............................. `↑` `↓`
3. Click `Insert` .... `Alt`+`N`

Remove Address

—IN ADDRESS BOOK—

1. Click desired address book tab .... `Ctrl`+`Tab`
2. Select address to remove.......................... `↑` `↓`

   NOTE: To select multiple addresses to delete, hold
   *down **Ctrl** and click each address.*

3. Click `Remove` .... `Alt`+`M`
4. Click `Yes` .... `↵`
   to confirm deletion.

Create Address List

Adds multiple addresses and names the group. You can then
insert all names in the group by selecting the group name.

—IN ADDRESS BOOK—

1. Click `Address List >>` .... `Alt`+`S`
2. Press **Ctrl** and click each address to add to group.
3. Click `Select Address:` .... `Alt`+`T`
4. Click `Save Group...` .... `Alt`+`G`
5. Type group name...*name*
6. Type **Comments** if desired .... `Alt`+`C`, *text*
7. Click `OK` .... `↵`

Create Personal Address Book

—IN ADDRESS BOOK—

1. Click **Boo<u>k</u>**, **<u>N</u>ew** .... `Ctrl`+`N`

2. Type address book **<u>N</u>ame**........................... *name*

3. Click | OK | .... `↵`

*A tab for your new, personal address book appears with the My Addresses and Frequent Contacts tabs in the **Corel Address Book window**.*

Delete Address Book

—IN ADDRESS BOOK—

1. Click **Boo<u>k</u>**, **De<u>l</u>ete**.......................... `Alt`+`K`, `L`

2. Select address book to delete................... `↑` `↓`

3. Click | OK | .... `↵`

4. Click | <u>Y</u>es | .... `↵`
   to delete address book.

   OR

   Click | <u>N</u>o | .... `Alt`+`N`
   to cancel deletion.

   NOTE: *You cannot delete **My Addresses** or **Frequent Contacts** from the Corel Address Book.*

Hide Address Book

—IN ADDRESS BOOK—

1. Click tab of address book to close......... `Ctrl`+`Tab`

2. Click **Boo<u>k</u>**, **<u>C</u>lose** .... `Ctrl`+`F4`

Display Hidden Address Book

—IN ADDRESS BOOK—

1. Click **Book**, **Open** .... `Ctrl`+`O`

2. Select address book to display.................. `↑` `↓`

3. Click [OK] .... `↵`

BOLD

Bold Existing Text

1. Select text to boldface.

2. Click **Bold** `B` .... `Ctrl`+`B`

Bold New Text

1. Click **Bold** `B` to turn bold on .... `Ctrl`+`B`

2. Type text .... *text*

3. Click **Bold** `B` to turn bold off .... `Ctrl`+`B`

BOOKMARKS

*Holds your place in a document. You must create a name for each bookmark except the **QuickMark** bookmark. The QuickMark bookmark is always named **QuickMark**. Use it to quickly create a bookmark without having to name it.*

Create Bookmark

1. Place cursor where bookmark is to appear.
   OR
   Select text to mark.

2. Click **Tools**, **Bookmark**..................... `Alt`+`T`, `B`

3. Click [Create...] .... `Alt`+`E`

continued...

CREATE BOOKMARK (CONTINUED)

4. Type **Bookmark Name**..................................... *text*
   if necessary.

5. Click `OK` .... `↵`

Go to Bookmark

1. Click **Tools**, **Bookmark** .... `Alt`+`T`, `B`

2. Select bookmark to find .... `↓` `↑`

   To go to bookmark:

   Click `Go To` .... `Alt`+`G`

   To go to bookmark and select text:

   Click `Go To & Select` .... `Alt`+`S`

   *NOTE: The **Go To & Select** button is available only
   if you selected a block of text when you
   created the bookmark.*

Set QuickMark

1. Place cursor where you wish to insert QuickMark.
   OR
   Select text to mark with Quickmark.

2. Click **Tools**, **Bookmark** .... `Alt`+`T`, `B`

3. Click `Set QuickMark` .... `Alt`+`Q`

   *NOTE: You can have only one QuickMark in
   a document.*

Go to QuickMark

1. Click **Tools**, **Bookmark** .... `Alt`+`T`, `B`

2. Click `Find QuickMark` .... `Alt`+`F`

WordPerfect

BORDERS/FILLS

Add Column Border/Fill

1. Place cursor anywhere in column.

2. Click **For̲mat**, **C̲olumns** .... `Alt`+`R`, `C`

3. Click | Bo̲rder/Fill... | .... `Alt`+`R`

4. Select desired border .... `↑` `↓` `←` `→`

5. Select desired **C̲olor**, **L̲ine style**, and/or **D̲rop shadow**.

6. If desired, deselect **Appl̲y** .... `Alt`+`Y`
   border to current column group only.

7. Click | Fill | .... `Ctrl`+`Tab`

8. Select desired fill .... `↑` `↓` `←` `→`

9. Select desired **F̲oreground**, **B̲ackground**, and/or **P̲attern**.

10. Click | OK | twice .... `↵`, `↵`

Add Paragraph Border/Fill

1. Place cursor in paragraph to format.
   OR
   Select paragraph(s) to format.

2. Click **For̲mat**, **P̲aragraph** .... `Alt`+`R`, `A`

3. Click **B̲order/Fill** .... `B`

4. Select desired border .... `↑` `↓` `←` `→`

5. Select desired **C̲olor**, **L̲ine style**, and/or **D̲rop shadow**.

continued...

ADD PARAGRAPH BORDER/FILL (CONTINUED)

6. If desired, deselect **Apply border**............ `Alt`+`Y`
   to current paragraph only.

7. Click [Fill] .... `Ctrl`+`Tab`

8. Select desired fill.............................. `↑` `↓` `←` `→`

9. Select desired **Foreground**, **Background**,
   and/or **Pattern**.

10. Click [OK] .... `↵`

Add Page Border/Fill

1. Place cursor on first page to format.

2. Click **Format**, **Page**........................ `Alt`+`R`, `P`

3. Click **Border/Fill**..................................... `B`

4. Select **Border type**............................ `F4`, `↑` `↓`

5. Select desired border .... `Alt`+`V`, `↑` `↓` `←` `→`

   If you selected Line in step 4:

   a. Select desired **Color**, **Line style**, and/or
      Drop shadow.

   b. Click **Rounded corners**....................... `Alt`+`R`
      to select, if desired.

   c. If desired, select **Apply border** .... `Alt`+`Y`
      to current page only.

   d. Click [Fill] .... `Ctrl`+`Tab`

   e. Select desired fill.................... `↑` `↓` `←` `→`

   f. Select desired **Foreground**, **Background**,
      and/or **Pattern**.

6. Click [OK] .... `↵`

WordPerfect

Customize Border/Fill

1. Complete steps 1–3 of appropriate
   BORDERS/FILLS procedure, preceding pages.

2. Select border/fill to customize.

3. Click `Advanced` .... `Ctrl`+`Tab`

   NOTE: *In **Page Border/Fill** dialog box, this tab is*
   *available only for **Line** border styles.*

4. Select desired options.

   NOTE: *Available options depend on the type of*
   border you are customizing.

5. Click `OK` .... `↵`
   to return to document.

Turn Off Border

1. Place cursor where you will end border.

2. Click **Format** .... `Alt`+`R`

3. Click **Paragraph**, **Page**, or **Columns**, as needed.

4. Click **Border/Fill** .... `B`
   for paragraphs/pages.

   OR

   Click `Border/Fill...` .... `Alt`+`R`
   for columns.

5. Click `Discontinue` .... `Alt`+`D`

6. Click `OK` .... `↵`
   if necessary.

BULLETS AND NUMBERS

Apply Bullets and Numbers

1. Select paragraph(s) to bullet or number.

   OR

   Position cursor where you will begin adding bullets or numbers to new paragraphs that you type (automatic bullets/numbering).

2. Click **Insert** .... `Alt`+`I`

3. Click **Outline/Bullets & Numbering** .... `N`

4. Click `Numbers` or `Bullets` .... `Ctrl`+`Tab`

5. Select desired bullet .... `↑``↓``←``→`
   or number style.

   *NOTE: For additional bullet symbols, click the **More bullets** button. Select desired symbol **Set**. Next, select desired bullet from **Symbols** and click the **Insert and Close** button.*

   To turn on automatic bullets/numbering:

   Click **Start new outline or list** .... `Alt`+`S`

6. Click `OK` .... `↵`

Turn Off Automatic Bullets/Numbering

1. Press **Enter** .... `↵`
   in last paragraph to apply bullets or numbers.

2. Press **Backspace** .... `Backspace`

CENTER

Center Text

Use this procedure, for example, to center a title or heading.

1. Place cursor where alignment is to begin.

2. Click **Justification** [icon] .... `Shift`+`F7`
   and select [icon] Center

   NOTE: *To center text with a dot leader, press*
   ***Shift+F7** twice.*

3. Type text, if necessary .... *text*

Center Paragraph

1. Select paragraph(s) to center.

   OR

   Position cursor where you will turn on centering for
   following paragraphs.

2. Click **Fo_r_mat**, **_J_ustification** .... `Alt`+`R`, `J`

3. Click **C_e_nter** .... `E`

Center Page (Top to Bottom)

1. Place cursor in first page to center.

2. Click **Fo_r_mat**, **_P_age**, **_C_enter** ..... `Alt`+`R`, `P`, `C`

3. Click **Current _p_age** .... `P`

   OR

   Click **Current and _s_ubsequent pages** .... `S`

4. Click [OK] .... `⏎`

CLOSE

Close Document

Click **File**, **Close** .... `Ctrl`+`F4`

If Save changes to Document message appears:

Click `Yes` .... `↵`
to save document and close.

OR

Click `No` .... `N`
to close document without saving changes.

If Save As or File Save dialog box appears:

a. Type **File name** .... *name*

> NOTE: *To select a different folder in which to save file, click Save in and select desired folder.*

b. Click `Save` .... `↵`

Close (Exit) WordPerfect

1. Click **File**, **Exit** .... `Alt`+`F4`

If Save changes to Document message appears:

Click `Yes` .... `↵`
to save changes and exit.

OR

Click `No` .... `N`
to exit without saving changes.

> NOTE: *If Save As or File Save dialog box appears, type File name, select folder to Save in, and click the Save button.*

2. Repeat above steps for each document to close.

COLUMNS

Column Types

- **Newspaper** — Flows down to the bottom of the first column and up to the top of the next one.

- **Balanced Newspaper** — Same as Newspaper except that each column is of equal length.

- **Parallel** — Groups text across the page in rows. The next row starts below the longest column of the previous row.

- **Parallel w/ block protect** — Keeps each row of columns together on a page. If a column in one row becomes so long it moves to the next page, the entire row moves with it.

Define/Turn On Columns

1. Place cursor where columns are to begin.

2. Click **Format**, **Columns** .... `Alt`+`R`, `C`

3. Type desired **Number of columns** .... *number*

4. Select desired **Type of columns** option.

   To set default space between columns:

   a. Click **Space between** columns .... `Alt`+`S`

   b. Type desired measurement .... *number*

   To set space between rows in parallel columns:

   a. Click **Extra line spacing** .... `Alt`+`E`
   in parallel columns.

   b. Type or desired measurement .... *number*

5. Change **Column widths** settings, if desired.

   NOTE: Use these settings to set up columns of unequal widths.

6. Click ⌷ OK ⌷ .... `⏎`

Insert Column Break

Press **Ctrl+Enter** .... Ctrl + ⏎

Turn Off Columns

1. Place cursor where columns are to end.

2. Click **Columns** ▦ .... Alt + R , C

3. Click ⌷Discontinue⌷ .... Alt + D

   OR

   Select **Discontinue** from **Columns** ▦ drop-down list on toolbar.

Delete Column Definition

1. Turn on Reveal Codes .... Alt + F3

2. Place cursor directly after column definition code: ⌷Col Def⌷

3. Press **Backspace** .... Backspace

Move from Column to Column

TO MOVE:	PRESS:
To top of column	Alt + Home
To last line of column	Alt + End
To previous column	Alt + ←
To next column	Alt + →

COMMENTS

Create Comment

1. Position cursor where comment marker will appear.

   NOTE: *If you add your initials (See **Set Initials/Color for Comments**), they will display in the left margin next to the comment.*

2. Click **I**nsert, Co**m**ment .... `Alt`+`I`, `M`

3. Click **C**reate .... `C`

4. Type comment .... *text*

5. Press **Ctrl+F4** to close window .... `Ctrl`+`F4`

Comment initials or icon (⬚) display(s) in margin. The comment is attached to the text where the cursor was positioned when you created the comment and moves along with text.

View Comment

Click comment mark icon ⬚

Set Initials/Color for Comments

Use this procedure to mark your comments with your initials and/or to show different peoples comments in different colors. You can distribute a copy of the document with each reviewer's comments marked by his/her initials and different colors.

1. Click **T**ools, Setti**n**gs .... `Alt`+`T`, `N`

2. Double-click [Environment] .... `Alt`+`E`, `↵`

3. Click [General] .... `Ctrl`+`Tab`

continued...

SET INITIALS/COLOR FOR COMMENTS (CONTINUED)

4. Type your **Initials** to mark your... `Alt`+`I` ,*initials*
   comments with your initials, if desired.

5. Click **User Color** `📇`... `Alt`+`L`, `F4`, `↑`, `↓`, `↵`
   to set the color for your comments, if desired.

6. Click `OK`

7. Click `Close` .... `Alt`+`C`

Show/Hide Comments

1. Click **Tools**, **Settings** .... `Alt`+`T`, `N`

2. Double-click `Display` .... `↵`

3. Click `Document` .... `Ctrl`+`Tab`

4. Click **Comments** check box .... `C`

   *NOTE: When this check box is selected,
   comments are displayed in document.*

5. Click `OK` .... `↵`

6. Click `Close` .... `Alt`+`C`

Edit Comment

1. Right-click comment.

2. Click **Edit** .... `E`

3. Change comment as desired.

4. Press **Ctrl+F4** to close window .... `Ctrl`+`F4`

Delete Comment

1. Right-click comment.

2. Click **Delete** .... `D`

WordPerfect 17

CONVERT CASE

Converts text to upper– or lowercase letters.

> *NOTE:* *When converting to initial capitals, words like "and" and "the" remain in lowercase. When converting to lowercase, words starting with "I" (e.g., "I'd," "I'm," etc.) and the first word of each sentence remain(s) uppercase.*

1. Select text to convert.
2. Click **Edit**, **Convert Case** .... `Alt` + `E`, `V`
3. Select desired option .... `↑` `↓`, `↵`

COPY/MOVE DATA

Copy or Cut to Clipboard

Information stays on the Clipboard until you paste it into another WordPerfect document or another Windows application.

1. Select text and/or graphics box.
2. Click **Copy** 🖺 to copy data .... `Ctrl` + `C`
   OR
   Click **Cut** ✂ to cut data .... `Ctrl` + `X`
   OR
   Click **Edit**, **Append** to append .... `Alt` + `E`, `A`
   to data already in the Clipboard.
   > *NOTE:* *You can only append selected text (not a graphics box).*

Paste from Clipboard

1. Place cursor where you want to insert data.
2. Click **Paste** 🖺 .... `Ctrl` + `V`
   > *NOTE:* *Data remains on the Clipboard until you cut or copy another selection.*

Copy/Move Text Using Drag and Drop

Select text to copy/move.

To move text:

Drag selection to desired location.

To copy text:

a. Hold down **Ctrl** and drag selection to desired location.

b. Release the mouse button before releasing the **Ctrl** key.

CREATE DOCUMENT

Create Document Based on Default Template

Click **New Blank Document** 🗋 .... `Ctrl` + `N`

Create Document Based on Any Template

Templates *are documents that contain formatting for predefined types of documents, such as newsletters and reports.*

1. Click **File**, **New** .... `Ctrl` + `Shift` + `N`

2. Click drop-down arrow ▼ .... `F4`
   at top of dialog box to open
   list of template types.

3. Click desired template category .... `↑` `↓`, `↵`

   NOTE: *Displays available templates for the category that you selected. Since not all templates are added when you install WordPerfect, you may get a message that the desired template is unavailable. Rerun Setup to install the template.*

4. Double-click template .... `↑` `↓`, `↵`
   on which to base document.

   NOTE: *Some projects start a PerfectExpert that prompts you for information to create the document.*

WordPerfect

CROSS–REFERENCE

Create cross-references to pages, tables, graphics, titles, and other items. You must create three items to produce cross-references:

- **Reference**   Refers the reader to another section in the document.

- **Target**   The location to which you are referring the reader.

- **Target name**   The text that ties the reference and the target together. The reference and target are marked with the same target name. The target name is used only to generate cross-references; it is not printed.

To create cross-references, you must mark the references, targets, and target names. Then you must generate the cross-references. These procedures are outlined below.

Display Cross-Reference Bar

1. Click **Tools**, **Reference** .... `Alt`+`T`, `C`

2. Click **Cross-Reference** .... `C`

Mark Reference

—WITH CROSS-REFERENCE BAR DISPLAYED—

1. Place cursor where reference is to appear.

   NOTE: Type any necessary introductory text. For example, if the cross-reference is to a page, you might type "See also page...."

2. Click `Reference ▼` .... `Shift`+`Alt`+`R`

3. Select desired reference type .... `↑` `↓`, `↵`

MARK REFERENCE (CONTINUED)

4. Click [I̲arget: ▼] .... **Shift**+**Alt**+**T**

5. Select or type target name................... *target name*

   NOTE: The target name must be the same for the reference and the target. If you have not yet marked the target, the name will not appear in the list. Type the name and then mark the target.

6. Click [Mark R̲eference] .... **Shift**+**Alt**+**E**

   NOTES: A question mark (?) appears in the location of every cross-reference until you generate.

   Type any closing text or end punctuation, as necessary.

Mark Target

   —WITH CROSS–REFERENCE BAR DISPLAYED—

1. Place cursor immediately after target.

   NOTE: Turn on Reveal Codes, if necessary (Alt+F3).

2. Click [I̲arget: ▼] .... **Shift**+**Alt**+**T**

3. Select or type target name.................... *target name*

   NOTE: The target name must be the same for the target and the reference. If you created the target name when you marked the reference, it will appear in the list. Otherwise, type a name for the target.

4. Click [Mark Ta̲rget] .... **Shift**+**Alt**+**A**

WordPerfect 21

Generate Cross–References

> NOTE: A question mark (?) appears in the location
> of every cross–reference until you generate.
>
> Type any closing text or end punctuation,
> as necessary.

—WITH CROSS–REFERENCE BAR DISPLAYED—

1. Click `Generate...` .... `Shift`+`Alt`+`G`

2. Click `OK` .... `↵`

3. Click `Close` .... `Shift`+`Alt`+`C`
   to close Cross-Reference bar.

DATE/TIME

*Insert the date/time as text, or have it automatically update to
the current date/time each time you print the document.*

> NOTE: The date is determined by your computer
> clock. If the date displayed is incorrect,
> refer to your DOS or Windows
> documentation to reset the date and time
> on your computer.

Insert Date Using Default Format

1. Place cursor where you would like
   to place date.

2. Press **Ctrl+D** .... `Ctrl`+`D`
   to insert current date as text.

   OR

   Press **Ctrl+Shift+D** .... `Ctrl`+`Shift`+`D`
   to insert current date as a code to update
   automatically, if desired.

Insert Date/Time Using Predefined Format

1. Click **Insert**, **Date/Time** .... `Alt`+`I`,`D`

2. Select desired **Date/Time format** .... `↑`·`↓`

3. Click **Automatic update** .... `Alt`+`A`
   check box to insert as a code
   to update automatically, if desired.

4. Click [**Insert**] .... `↵`

DEFAULT DOCUMENT FOLDER

WordPerfect saves new documents and looks for documents to open in the default document folder.

1. Click **Tools**, **Settings** .... `Alt`+`T`,`N`

2. Double-click **Files** .... `Alt`+`F`,`↵`

3. Click [Document] .... `Ctrl`+`Tab`

4. Type **Default document** .... `Alt`+`D`,*pathname*
   folder pathname.

   OR

   Select desired **Default document folder**
   by clicking the **Browse** button.

5. Click [OK] .... `↵`

6. Click [Close] .... `Esc`

WordPerfect

DEFAULT DOCUMENT STYLE

*The default document style (called the **initial codes style** in previous versions of WordPerfect) sets the default formatting for the current document. You can also apply the document style to all new documents.*

> NOTE: This procedure can be completed at any time from anywhere within a WordPerfect document.

1. Click **File**, **Document** .... `Alt`+`F`, `D`

2. Click **Current Document Style** .... `D`

3. Set formatting options as desired.

4. Select **Use as default** to apply .... `Alt`+`U` formatting to all new documents, if desired.

5. Click `OK` .... `↵`

DELETE TEXT

TO DELETE:	PRESS:
Next character	`Delete`
Previous character	`Backspace`
To beginning of current word	`Ctrl`+`Backspace`
To end of line	`Ctrl`+`Delete`
To end of page	`Ctrl`+`Shift`+`Delete`
Selected text	`Delete`

ENVELOPES

Create Envelope for Existing Document

1. Open document and select address for envelope.
2. Click **Fo_r_mat, En_v_elope**.................. **Alt**+**R**, **V**

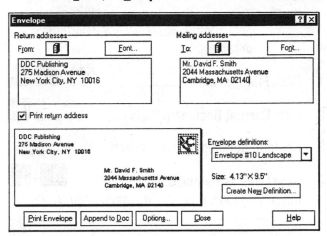

ENVELOPE DIALOG BOX

To change envelope definition:

Select desired definition ... **Alt**+**V**, **F4**, **↑**, **↓** from **En_v_elope definitions** list.

To add a return address or a mailing address:

Follow **Enter Envelope Address** procedure, below.

3. Print the envelope or insert it in the document:

To print envelope:

Click [**_P_rint Envelope**] .... **Alt**+**P**

To insert envelope definition at end of document:

Click [**Append to _D_oc**] .... **Alt**+**D**

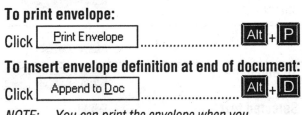

NOTE: You can print the envelope when you print the document.

WordPerfect   **25**

ENTER **E**NVELOPE **A**DDRESS

Enter a return address or a mailing address.

1. Follow **Create Envelope for Existing Document**, page 24.

   To type address:

   a. Select **F**r**o**m text box .... `Alt`+`R`
      for return address.

      AND/OR

      Select **T**o text box.............................. `Alt`+`T`
      for mailing address.

   b. Type address...*address*

   To select address from the Corel Address Book:

   *See **Address Book**, page 1, for information on adding addresses to the address book.*

   a. Click [📖] above **F**r**o**m text box (to enter return address) or **T**o text box (to enter mailing address).

   b. Select [🔄 My Addresses] or [🔄 Frequent Contacts] as necessary.

   c. Double-click desired address.

   d. Select desired address.

      OR

      Click [OK] .... `↵`

2. Click [**F**ont...] .... `Alt`+`F`
   to change return address font, if desired.

   AND/OR

   Click [Fo**n**t...] .... `Alt`+`N`
   to change mailing address font, if desired.

3. Select desired font option(s).

4. Click [OK] .... [↵]

   To insert bar code/adjust address position:

   a. Click [Options...] .... [Alt]+[S]

   b. Set options as desired.

   c. Click [OK] .... [↵]

5. Click [Close] .... [Alt]+[C]
   to exit dialog box.

Create Envelope Definition

To display Envelope dialog box:

Click **Format, Envelope** .... [Alt]+[R], [V]

1. Click [Create New Definition...] .... [Alt]+[W]

2. Type page definition **Name** .... *definition name*
   in text box.

3. Select desired **Size** ...... [Alt]+[Z], [F4], [↑], [↓], [↵]

4. Set other options, if necessary.

5. Click [OK] .... [↵]

6. Click [Close] .... [Alt]+[C]
   to exit dialog box.

FIND

QuickFind Selected Text

1. Select text to find.

2. Press **Alt+Ctrl+N** .... `Alt`+`Ctrl`+`N`
   to find next occurrence of text.

   OR

   Press **Alt+Ctrl+P** to find .... `Alt`+`Ctrl`+`P`
   previous occurrence of text.

Find Word(s) or Code(s)

1. Press **F2** .... `F2`

   *NOTE: If searching for codes, place cursor in
   Reveal Codes pane (**Alt+F3**).*

2. Type word(s) to find .... *word(s)*

   OR

   a. Click **Match**, **Codes** .... `Alt`+`M`,`O`
      to find code.

   b. Select desired code .... `↑``↓`
      in **Codes** dialog box.

   c. Click `Insert & Close` .... `Alt`+`N`

   OR

   a. Click **Type**, **Specific Codes** .... `Alt`+`T`,`S`
      to find occurrence of specific code.

   *NOTE: You can find more detailed code
   information, such as a 1" margin setting or
   a particular style name, with this option.*

   b. Select desired code .... `↑``↓`

continued...

FIND WORD(S) OR CODE(S) (CONTINUED)

   c Click [OK] .... ⏎

   d. Fill out options for information to find.

OR

   a. Click **Match**, **Font** .... Alt + M , F
      to find font codes.

   b. Click formatting attributes to find.

   c. Click [OK] .... ⏎

3. Complete procedure(s) below, as desired:

   To match whole words, case, or font of F̲ind text:

   a. Click **Match** .... Alt + M

   b. Select desired option(s)................ ↑ ↓ , ⏎

   To find word forms (e.g., "talk" "talking"):

   Click **T̲ype**, **W̲ord Forms**.......... Alt + T , W , ⏎

   To search entire document starting at cursor:

   a. Click **O̲ptions**.................................... Alt + O

   b. Click **W̲rap at Beg./End of Document**......... W

   To search selection only:

   a. Click **O̲ptions**.................................... Alt + O

   b. Click **L̲imit Find Within Selection** L

continued.

WordPerfect   29

4. Click `Find Next` .... `↵`
   to find next occurrence.

   OR

   Click `Find Prev` .... `Alt`+`P`
   to find previous occurrence.

5. Repeat step 4 as necessary.

6. Click `Close` .... `Esc`

Replace Word(s) or Code(s)

1. Complete steps 1–3 of **Find Word(s) or Code(s)**,
   page 27.

2. Type replacement text .... `Alt`+`W`, *text*
   in **Replace with** box.

   OR

   a. Click **Replace**, **Codes** .... `Alt`+`E`, `O`
      to replace code.

   b. Select desired code .... `↑` `↓`

   c. Click `Insert & Close` .... `Alt`+`N`

   OR

   a. Click **Type**, **Specific Codes** .... `Alt`+`T`, `S`
      to replace occurrence of specific code.

   *NOTE: For example, to replace a 1" bottom
            margin with a 1.5" bottom margin.*

   b. Select desired code .... `↑` `↓`

continued..

REPLACE WORD(S) OR CODE(S) (CONTINUED)

c. Click [OK] .... ⏎

d. Fill out options for information to find.

OR

a. Click **Replace, Font** .... Alt + E , F
   to replace font codes.

b. Click formatting attributes to replace.

c. Click [OK] .... ⏎

3. Click desired button:

   - [Find Next] .... ⏎

     *NOTE: Find Next and Find Prev allow you
     to select on a case–by–case basis
     to replace or not replace selected text.*

   - [Find Prev] .... Alt + P

   - [Replace] .... Alt + R

     *NOTE: The Replace button replaces the current
     selection only.*

   - [Replace All] .... Alt + A

   OR

   Click **Help, Help** .... Alt + H , ⏎

4. Click [Close] .... Esc

WordPerfect 31

FLUSH RIGHT

Flush Right Text

1. Place cursor where alignment is to begin.
2. Click **Justification** 🖺 .... `Alt`+`F7`
    then select `☰ Right`
3. Type text, if necessary .... *text*
4. Press **Enter** to end right alignment.................. `↵`

    NOTE: *If you use the Justification button, you*
    must click it again to deselect the feature.

Flush Right with Dot Leaders

1. Place cursor where alignment is to begin.
2   Press **Alt+F7** twice .... `Alt`+`F7`, `Alt`+`F7`
3. Type text .... *text*

Flush Right Existing Paragraphs

1. Select paragraph(s) to format.
2. Click **Justification** 🖺 .... `Ctrl`+`R`
    then select `☰ Right`

FONT

Show/Hide Font Toolbar

1. Click **View, Toolbars**...................... `Alt`+`V`, `T`
2. Click **Font** check box in list of **Available toolbars**.
3. Click `OK` .... `↵`

    NOTE: *Fonts displayed in the **Font Face** drop-down*
    list box are those currently installed for the
    selected printer.

Change Font Face, Style, and Size

1. Place cursor where font change is to begin.
    OR
    Select text to format.

2. Press **F9**... `F9`

3. Select desired options.

4. Click ⬛ OK ⬛ .... `↵`

Change Default Font for Printer

*Sets the default font for all documents created with the active printer. If you change the default font for a document (see **Set Default Font for Current Document**). the document default replaces the printer default.*

1. Press **Ctrl+P**..................................... `Ctrl`+`P`

2. Click ⬛ Details ⬛ .... `Ctrl`+`Tab`

3. Click ⬛ Default Font ⬛ .... `Alt`+`D`

4. Select desired font face, style, and size.

    NOTE: Not all font face selections have a variety of sizes and styles available.

5. Click ⬛ OK ⬛ .... `↵`

6. Click ⬛ Close ⬛ .... `Esc`

Set Default Font for Current Document

1. Click **Format**, **Font**................................... `F9`

2. Click ⬛ Default Font... ⬛ .... `Alt`+`T`

3. Click **Use as default** to deselect it .... `Alt`+`U`

4. Select desired font face, style, and size.

5. Click ⬛ OK ⬛ twice.............................. `↵`, `↵`

FOOTNOTES AND ENDNOTES

> *NOTES:* When you add and delete
> footnotes/endnotes, WordPerfect
> automatically renumbers existing
> notes, as necessary.
>
> WordPerfect also automatically
> recalculates the space necessary for
> footnote placement.

Create Footnote/Endnote

1. Place cursor where reference number should be placed.

2. Click **I**nsert, **F**ootnote/Endnote .... `Alt`+`I`, `F`

3. Type **F**ootnote Number .... `Alt`+`F`,*number*

    OR

    Type E**n**dnote Number .... `Alt`+`N`,*number*

4. Click `Create` .... `↵`

5. Type note text .... *text*

6. Click in document to exit footnote area if you are working in Page view.

    OR

    Click **Ctrl+F4** if working in Draft view ..... `Ctrl`+`F4`

Edit Footnote/Endnote

1. Click **I**nsert, **F**ootnote/Endnote .... `Alt`+`I`, `F`

2. Type desired note number .... *number*

3. Click `Edit` .... `Alt`+`E`

continued...

EDIT FOOTNOTE/ENDNOTE (CONTINUED)

4. Edit note text.

5. Click in document to exit footnote area if you are working in Page view.

   OR

   Click **Ctrl+F4** if working in Draft view ..... `Ctrl`+`F4`

Restart Footnote Numbering on Each Page

1. Click **I**nsert, **F**ootnote/Endnote....... `Alt`+`I`, `F`

2. Click **F**ootnote Number .... `Alt`+`F`
   to select it, if necessary.

3. Click `Options ▼` .... `Alt`+`O`, `F4`

4. Click **A**dvanced .... `A`

5. Click **R**estart numbering .... `Alt`+`R`
   on each page check box.

6. Click `OK` .... `↵`

7. Click `Close` .... `Esc`
   to close dialog box.

Renumber Footnote/Endnote

1. Click **I**nsert, **F**ootnote/Endnote....... `Alt`+`I`, `F`

2. Select **F**ootnote Number to change........ `Alt`+`F`

   OR

   Select **E**ndnote Number to change......... `Alt`+`N`

continued...

WordPerfect   35

3. Click `Options ▼` .... `Alt`+`O`, `F4`

4. Click **Set Number** .... `N`

5. Select numbering option as desired.

6. Click `OK` .... `⏎`

7. Click `Close` .... `Esc`
   to close dialog box.

Change Footnote/Endnote Mark

By default, WordPerfect numbers footnotes.

1. Click **Insert, Footnote/Endnote** .... `Alt`+`I`, `F`

2. Click **Footnote Number** .... `Alt`+`F`

   OR

   Click **Endnote Number** .... `Alt`+`N`

3. Click `Options ▼` .... `Alt`+`O`, `F4`

4. Click **Advanced** .... `A`

5. Click desired **Method** .... `F4`, `↑`, `↓`, `⏎`

   *NOTE: If you choose **Characters**, type **Characters**
   to use. For example, type *.*

6. Click `OK` .... `⏎`

7. Click `Close` .... `Esc`
   to close dialog box.

GENERATE

Updates lists, tables of contents, indexes, tables of authorities, and cross-references in the document.

> *NOTE: Each time you generate, all items in the document are generated or regenerated.*

1. Press **Ctrl+F9** .... `Ctrl`+`F9`

   If you have hypertext links in the document and wish to generate and save them:

   Click **B**uild hypertext links .... `B`

2. Click `OK` twice .... `↵`

GO TO

1. Press **Ctrl+G** .... `Ctrl`+`G`

   To go to top of specific page:

   Type desired **Page number** .... *page number*

   To go to specific position:

   a. Click **P**osition .... `Alt`+`P`

   b. Select desired position from list .... `↑` `↓`

   To go to specific bookmark:

   a. Click **B**ookmark .... `Alt`+`B`

   b. Select desired bookmark .... `F4`, `↑` `↓`
      from list.

   To go to top of specific table:

   a. Click **T**able .... `Alt`+`T`

   b. Select desired table from list .... `F4`, `↑` `↓`

continued...

To go to specific cell or range in table:

a. Click **T**able .... Alt + T

b. Select desired table from list .... F4, ↑ ↓

c. Click **C**ell/Range .... Alt + C

d. Type desired cell or range .... *cell* or *range*

2. Click [OK] .... ↵

GRAPHICS—CAPTIONS

*Captions for each type of graphics box that you create are numbered separately, if you number captions. For example, if you add captions to table graphic boxes and graphics image boxes (**graphics image boxes** contain clipart and pictures that you insert from a file), all tables will be numbered consecutively (such as **Table 3**) and all images will be numbered consecutively (such as **Figure 3**).*

Add/Edit Caption Text

1. Right-click graphic or text box.

2. Click **Create C**aption or **Edit C**aption C

   *NOTE: If the box already has a caption, the **Edit Caption** command appears on the pop-up menu instead of **Create Caption**.*

3. Create and/or edit caption text as desired .... *text*

4. Click outside caption to finish.

Edit Caption Settings

1. Right-click graphic or text box.

2. Click **Caption**..

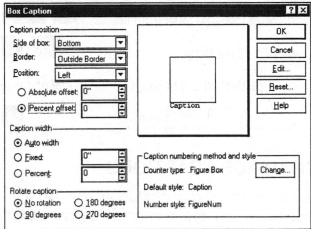

BOX CAPTION DIALOG BOX

To remove caption numbering:

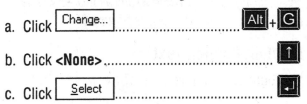

a. Click ⌐Change...⌐ .... Alt + G

b. Click **<None>** .... ↑

c. Click ⌐Select⌐ .... ↵

To place the caption:

NOTE: The preview window shows the selected caption placement.

a. Select **Side of box** option to specify which side of the graphic the caption will appear on.

b. Select **Border** option to place caption inside or outside of the border.

continued.

c. Select **<u>P</u>osition** option to align the caption in relation to the box.

d. Type **Abso<u>l</u>ute offset** measurement to shift the caption from its current position.

> *NOTE: Type a negative number (such as -.25")*
> *to move the caption to the left. Type a*
> *positive number (such as .5") to move*
> *the caption to the right.*

OR

Type **Percent <u>o</u>ffset** number to shift the caption by a percentage of the size of the box.

> *NOTE: For example, you could shift the caption*
> *the amount of space equal to 10% of the*
> *size of the box.*

3. Select other option(s) as desired.

> *NOTE: To view a pop-up description of an option,*
> *click ☐? in title bar, then click option.*

4. Click [OK] .... [↵]

Delete Caption

1. Right-click graphic or text box.

2. Click **<u>C</u>aption** .... [A]

3. Click [<u>R</u>eset...] .... [Alt]+[R]

4. Click [OK] twice .... [↵],[↵]

GRAPHICS—CREATE AND INSERT

NOTE:　For many of the procedures below, the Graphics Box Edit Box must be displayed. If it is not displayed, press Alt+G, E.

Insert Picture File

1.　Click **I**nsert, **G**raphics..... .... `Alt`+`I` `G`

2.　Click **F**rom File.. `F`

3.　Double-click file to insert.

Insert Clip Art

1.　Click **I**nsert, **G**raphics.................... `Alt`+`I` `G`

2.　Click **C**lipart .... `C`

3.　Display clipart picture to insert.

　　*NOTE:　If you have your Corel installation CD, you can click the **CD Clipart** tab to view more pictures.*

4.　Drag clipart picture from Scrapbook to document.

5.　Click ⊠ in title bar to close Scrapbook.

Create TextArt

*See **TEXTART**, page 128.*

Create Text Box

*Use a text box to place text anywhere in the document by dragging the box on the page. A **text box** is a type of graphics box. By default, a text box has a border around it.*

1. Drag on page to size of new text box.

A broken line shows the outline of the new text box:

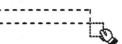

2. Release mouse button.

The following menu appears:

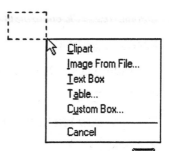

    Clipart
    Image From File...
    Text Box
    Table...
    Custom Box...

    Cancel

3. Click **Text Box** ....

4. Type text .... *text*

    NOTE: If the text box is too small for you to see text as you type, you can resize the box. (See **Resize Graphic or Text Box**, page 42.)

5. Click outside box to finish.

Rotate Text in Text Box

1. Right-click text box.

2. Click **Content** .... N

3. Click desired **Rotate text counterclockwise** option.

4. Click [OK] .... ↵

Format Characters in Text Box

1. Drag across text to format.
2. Press **F9**.. `F9`
3. Set options as desired.
4. Click `OK` .... ↵

Resize Graphic or Text Box

If resizing a text box, text wraps to fit the new size. If resizing a graphic, resize the entire graphic (not just the graphics box).

RESIZE USING MENU

1. Right-click graphic or text box.
2. Click **Size** .... `Z`
3. Type new **Width** and **Height** measurements.
4. Click `OK` .... ↵

RESIZE USING MOUSE

1. Click on graphic or outside border of text box.

Small boxes, called handles, appear around the box.

2. Position cursor over a handle until the pointer changes to a two-headed arrow.

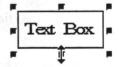

3. Drag to resize.

Move Graphic or Text Box

1. Click outside border of graphic or text box.

*Small boxes, called **handles**, appear around the box and the pointer changes to a crossbar.*

2. Drag to new position.

Delete Graphic or Text Box

1. Click outside border of graphic or text box.

   NOTE: When object is selected, black handles appear around it.

2. Press **Delete** or **Backspace** .... or

Attach Graphic or Text Box to Text

*Attach to a paragraph, a page, or treat it as a character in a line of text (the graphic moves with surrounding text just as though it were a character, called an **in-line graphic**).*

1. Right-click graphic or text box.

2. Click **P**osition.. [P]

3. Select **A**ttach box to.................... [F4], [↑], [↓], [↵]
   option as follows:

   - **Page**   Stays with page, even if information is added and/or deleted.

   - **Paragraph**   Stays with paragraph. If information is added to push paragraph to next page, box moves to next page also.

   - **Character**   Box is treated just like a single character of text, staying in its place in the line of text.

4. Set other options to position precisely as desired.

   NOTE: Placement options depend on the attachment option selected in step 3.

5. Click [OK] .... [↵]

Display Image Tools

Use image tools to rotate, move, edit, and otherwise customize a graphic. You cannot use image tools with text boxes.

1. Right-click graphic.

2. Click **Image Tools** ....

   NOTE: *To display a description of a tool, click [?] in the **Image Tools** dialog box title bar, then click the tool button. To close description, click off of the **Image Tools** dialog box.*

Rotate Image

—WITH IMAGE TOOLS DISPLAYED—

1. Click [Rotate] ....[Alt]+[R]

2. Drag ✚ to new location if desired.

   NOTE: *This icon marks the center of rotation. When you rotate the graphic, it will rotate around this point. Moving this icon changes the center of rotation.*

3. Drag ⟳ to rotate.

4. Click outside graphics box to return to document.

Change Text Flow Around Graphic or Text Box

1. Right-click graphic or text box.

2. Click **Wrap** .... [R]

continued...

CHANGE TEXT FLOW AROUND GRAPHIC (CONTINUED)

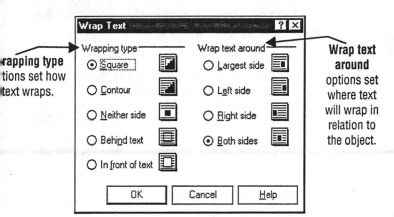

Wrapping type tions set how text wraps.

Wrap text around options set where text will wrap in relation to the object.

WRAP TEXT DIALOG BOX

NOTE: To display a description of a wrap option, click ? in title bar, then click option. To close description, click elsewhere.

3. Select desired **Wrapping type** option.

4. Select desired **Wrap text around** option.

5. Click ☐ OK .... ⏎

Apply/Remove Borders or Fill

1. Right-click graphic or text box.

2. Click **Border/Fill**.. B

3. Click desired border style............. ↑ ↓ ← →

4. Select desired **Color**, **Line style**, and/or **Drop shadow**.

continued…

5. Click [Apply] to view border............... [Alt]+[A]
   applied to graphic or text box
   without exiting dialog box.

   *NOTE: You may need to move the **Box Border/Fill**
   dialog box to view the effect.*

6. Click [Fill] .... [Ctrl]+[Tab]

7. Click fill style to apply.................. [↑][↓][←][→]

8. Select desired **Foreground**,
   Background, and/or **Pattern**.

9. Click [Apply] to view fill .... [Alt]+[A]
   applied to graphic or text box
   without exiting dialog box.

10. Click [OK].. [↵]

Edit Graphics Box

*When you insert a graphic, WordPerfect automatically adds a
graphics box to hold the graphic. Graphics box settings
depend on the type of graphic that you insert. You cannot see
the graphics box in most cases because most graphics boxes
do not have borders (by default text boxes, and some other
types of graphics boxes do, however, have borders by default).
Use this procedure to view or change graphics box settings.*

1. Right-click box.

2. Click **Edit Box** .... [O]

3. Set options as desired.

   *NOTE: To view a pop-up description of an option,
   right-click the option.*

4. Click [OK] .... [↵]

HARD SPACE

Inserts a special space character that keeps two words together on a line (e.g., full names, dates). If the second word does not fit on the line, both words wrap to the next line.

1. Place cursor where you would like to insert hard a space.

2. Delete existing space, if necessary .... Delete

3. Click **Fo**r**mat**, **L**ine .... Alt + R , L

4. Click **O**ther **Codes** .... O

5. Click **Hard space [HSpace]** .... Alt + P

6. Click Insert .... ↵

HEADERS AND FOOTERS

> NOTE: *Headers and footers are visible only in Page view and Two Pages view.*

Create Header/Footer

1. Place cursor on first page where header or footer is to appear.

2. Click **I**nsert, **H**eader/Footer .... Alt + I , H

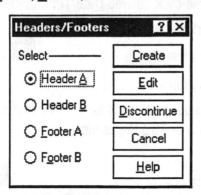

HEADERS/FOOTERS DIALOG BOX

continued...

CREATE HEADER/FOOTER (CONTINUED)

3. Select header or footer to create.

   NOTE: You can have two headers and two footers on a page.

4. Click ⌷ Create ⌷ .... ⌷↵⌷

5. Type and format header/footer text .... *text*
   as desired.

   To insert page number:

   a. Click **Fo__r__mat**, **__P__age** .... ⌷Alt⌷+⌷R⌷, ⌷P⌷

   b. Click **__I__nsert Page Number** .... ⌷I⌷

   c. Click number to insert .... ⌷↑⌷ ⌷↓⌷

   d. Click ⌷ Insert ⌷ .... ⌷↵⌷

   e. Click ⌷ __C__lose ⌷ .... ⌷Alt⌷+⌷C⌷

   To insert date/time:

   a. Click **__I__nsert**, **__D__ate/Time** .... ⌷Alt⌷+⌷I⌷, ⌷D⌷

   b. Select **__K__eep the inserted** .... ⌷Alt⌷+⌷K⌷
      date current check box if you want
      date to update each time you print.

   c. Double-click desired **__D__ate/Time format** to insert.

   To insert filename:

   a. Click **__I__nsert**, **__O__ther** .... ⌷Alt⌷+⌷I⌷, ⌷O⌷

   b. Click **__F__ilename** .... ⌷F⌷

6. Click in document body text to exit header/footer in
   Page view or Two Pages view.

   OR

   Press **Ctrl+F4** .... ⌷Ctrl⌷+⌷F4⌷
   to exit header/footer mode in Draft view.

WordPerfect

Suppress Header/Footer on Page

1. Place cursor on page where you do not want header/footer to print.

2. Click **For̲mat**, **P̲age** .... Alt + R , P

3. Click **S̲uppress** .... U

4. Click item(s) to **Suppress on current page**.

   NOTE: *If you have page numbers in the header/footer that you want to suppress, select **P̲age numbering** in addition to headers/footers to suppress.*

5. Click OK .... ↵

Discontinue Header/Footer

Use this procedure to turn off header/footer so that it does not appear on subsequent pages.

   NOTE: *To start a different header/footer, first end the previous header/footer and then follow the **Create Header/Footer** procedure to create a new header/footer.*

1. Place cursor on page where you want to end a header/footer.

2. Click **I̲nsert**, **H̲eader/Footer** .... Alt + I , H

3. Select header/footer to end.

4. Click D̲iscontinue .... Alt + D

5. Repeat steps 2–4 to end other headers and/or footers as desired.

Delete Header/Footer

1. Use the **Find** feature to locate the code to delete. (*See* **Find**, *page 27.*)

   NOTE: *Codes to search for are: [Header A], [Header B], [Footer A], and/or [Footer B].*

2. Drag code to delete out of **Reveal Codes** window.

HYPERLINKS

Use hyperlinks in online documents (such as Web pages) to jump from one part of a document to another part of the same document or to a different document entirely. You can also use a hyperlink to run a macro. When you click on a hyperlink, the referenced document/location displays or the macro runs.

*When you create a hyperlink, you link to an existing **bookmark** in the current document or another document. The bookmark marks the target location. (See **Bookmarks**, page 5, for more information.) If you convert a document to HTML format for use on the Web, bookmarks are converted to HTML anchors.*

*Hyperlinks can be in two basic styles: **highlighted words**, **phrases**, **or objects** and **hypertext buttons**. When you create hypertext links, you use the **Hypertext feature bar**.*

Create Hyperlink

1. Select text or object to use as link.

   NOTE: *This is the text or object that you will click to go to the hyperlink destination. If you use text, you can have the text appear as a button in the document if desired. If you use a graphic as a hyperlink and convert the document to HTML, WordPerfect converts the graphic to Web format.*

2. Click **Tools**, **Hyperlink**.................... Alt + T , Y

continued...

WordPerfect   51

3. Specify hyperlink destination or macro
    using one of the following procedures:

    To link to Web page:

    Type Web **Document** address .... *address*

    OR

    Click Browse Web... .... **Alt** + **W**
    to select destination address.

    *NOTE: This command starts your Web browser so
               you can connect to the Internet. The
               address of the displayed Web page appears
               in the **Document/Macro** text box.*

    To link to a different document:

    Type **Document** filename .... *path/filename*
    including path.

    To link to specific location:

    Type or select **Bookmark** ..... **Alt** + **B**, **F4**, **↑**, **↓**

    *NOTES: To link to a specific location in an HTML
             document, type the HTML anchor name.
             First, bookmark the destination location.
             For example, to create a hyperlink that
             jumps to a Table of Contents, mark the
             top of that page with a bookmark.*

    *To link to a location in the current
    document, the **Document/Macro** text box
    should be set to **<current document>** (the
    default setting).*

    To run a macro:

    Type **Macro** name ....*name*
    in **Document/Macro** text box.

    *NOTE: Do not use this feature in documents that you
               intend to place on the Internet as not all Web
               browsers can run WordPerfect macros.*

continued...

CREATE HYPERLINK (CONTINUED)

4. Click **Make text appear as a button** .... `Alt`+`M`
    check box to create a button from
    text selected in step 1, if desired.

5. Click **Activate hyperlinks** check box....... `Alt`+`A`
    to enable/disable all hyperlinks in document.

> *NOTE:*   *If hyperlinks are deactivated, clicking on*
> *them does not jump to the destination or*
> *run the macro.*

6. Click `OK` .... `⏎`

Edit Link

1. Right-click hyperlink.

2. Click **Edit Hyperlink**......................... `Y`,`Y`,`⏎`

3. Change options as desired.

4. Click `OK` .... `⏎`

Edit Hyperlink Button

Use procedures in **GRAPHICS—CREATE AND INSERT**
section, page 40.

Delete Hyperlink

DELETE TEXT HYPERLINK:

1. Drag across text to select it.

2. Press **Delete** .... `Delete`

DELETE BUTTON OR GRAPHIC HYPERLINK:

1. Right-click button or graphic.

2. Click **Delete Box**.............................. `L`

WordPerfect   53

HYPHENATION

Turn Hyphenation On/Off

> NOTE: Hyphenate just before you print so that you
> are not interrupted by hyphenation
> prompts as you type.

1. Place cursor where you will begin hyphenating.

2. Click **Tools**, **Language** .... `Alt`+`T`,`U`

3. Click **Hyphenation** .... `H`

4. Click to select/deselect **Turn hyphenation on** .... `O`
   check box.

5. Increase/decrease **Hyphenation zone** using
   increment arrows (also known as *spin buttons*) 🔼
   or enter percentage(s) in **Percent left** and/or
   Percent right text boxes.

   > NOTE: Only words that fall within the hyphenation
   > zone are hyphenated.

6. Click ⟦ OK ⟧ .... `↵`

*The word requiring hyphenation is displayed with a suggested
hyphen position. Select option as desired. To display a
description of a button, click* `?` *in title bar, then click button.
To close description, click elsewhere.*

Insert Hard Hyphen

*Inserts a special hyphen that keeps words together on a line
(e.g., phone numbers and hyphenated dates). If the second
word does not fit on a line, both words wrap to the next line.*

Press **Ctrl+ –** .... `Ctrl`+`–`

INDENT

1. Place cursor where indent is to begin.

   OR

   Select paragraph(s) to indent.

2. Indent text using one of the following procedures:

   To indent left side of paragraph to next tab stop:

   Click **Fo_r_mat**, **P_a_ragraph**, **_I_ndent**.................... `F7`

   To indent all lines (except first) to next tab stop:

   Click **Fo_r_mat**,................................ `Ctrl`+`F7`
   P_a_ragraph, **_H_anging Indent**.

   To indent left and right side one tab stop:

   Click **Fo_r_mat**,........................ `Ctrl`+`Shift`+`F7`
   P_a_ragraph, **_D_ouble Indent**.

   NOTE: *To align only the first line of text with the previous tab stop, click Fo_r_mat, P_a_ragraph, Back _T_ab.*

3. Press **Enter** .... `↵`
   after typing new paragraph text
   to end paragraph and indenting.

INDEX

To create an index, you must complete the following three steps:

- *Create a **concordance file** and/or **mark items** to include in the index.*
- ***Define** the index style and location.*
- ***Generate** the index.*

Show Index Feature Bar

Use the Index feature bar to mark the items to include in the index, to define the index, and to generate it.

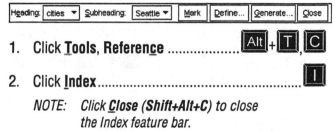

1. Click **Tools, Reference** .... **Alt** + **T**, **C**

2. Click **Index** .... **I**

    *NOTE: Click **Close (Shift+Alt+C)** to close the Index feature bar.*

Create Concordance File

*A **concordance file** is a list of words and phrases WordPerfect uses to generate an index. WordPerfect searches your document for each entry in the concordance file and inserts the entry and its page number in the index.*

1. Open new document.

2. Type entry for index .... *index entry*

    NOTE: For example, if you want to include the word "maps" in your index, enter it in the concordance file.

3. Press **Enter** .... ⏎

4. Repeat steps 2 and 3 for each index entry.

5. Save and name the document.

Mark Index Entries

—WITH INDEX FEATURE BAR ACTIVE—

1. Create heading/subheading using one of the two procedures below:

   NOTE: *A heading is a first-level index entry, such as "cities" in the example below. A subheading is a second-level entry such as "Seattle." Example:*

   > *cities*
   > > *Miami*
   > > *Seattle*
   > > *Tacoma*

   a. Select word(s) in document to include in index.

   b. Click **H_eading** ....`Shift`+`Alt`+`E`/`S`
      and/or **S_ubheading**.

   OR

   a. Position cursor next to text to mark.

   b. Type or select word(s)... `Shift`+`Alt`+`E`/`S`,*text*
      in **H_eading** and/or
      S_ubheading text box(es).

2. Click `M_ark` ....`Shift`+`Alt`+`M`

3. Repeat steps 1-2 to mark all headings/subheadings.

Define Index

—WITH INDEX FEATURE BAR ACTIVE—

1. Place cursor where index is to appear.

2. Type title, if desired (e.g., *INDEX*) ....*title*

3. Press **Enter** ....`↵`

4. Click `D_efine...` ....`Shift`+`Alt`+`D`

continued.

To specify page numbering position:

Select desired **Position** option ... `F4`, `↑`, `↓`, `↵`

To change page numbering format:

a. Click `Page Numbering...` .... `Alt`+`N`

b. Click **Document page**......................... `Alt`+`D`
   number format check box to include
   document page numbers only.

   OR

   i. Click `Insert ▼` .... `Alt`+`I`

   ii. Select desired custom...... `F4`, `↑`, `↓`, `↵`
       number format options.

c. Click `OK` .... `↵`
   to exit **Page Number Format** dialog box.

**To see each number printed (e.g., 20, 21, 22)
instead of combined (e.g., 20–22):**

Deselect **Use dash to show**................... `Alt`+`U`
consecutive pages check box.

To change heading and subheading style:

a. Click `Change...` .... `Alt`+`C`

b. Select index style to change................. `↑` `↓`

c. Click `Edit` .... `Alt`+`E`

d. Format style as desired.

e. Click `OK` to close **Styles Editor** dialog box.

f. Click `OK` .... `↵`
   to exit **Index Styles** dialog box.

continued...

DEFINE INDEX (CONTINUED)

If you are using a concordance file:

a. Click **Filename** text box............ ...... [Alt] + [F]

b. Click the **Browse** button [🖿] to select the drive, folder, and filename of the concordance file in the **Select Concordance File** dialog box.

c. Click the **Select** button .... [↵]

5. Click [OK] .... [↵]
   to close the **Define Index** dialog box.

<<Index will generate here>> appears beneath your title.

Generate Index

—WITH INDEX FEATURE BAR ACTIVE—

1. Click [Generate...] .... [Shift] + [Alt] + [G]

2. Click [OK] .... [↵]

> *NOTE: To format the index in multiple (newspaper) columns, see **COLUMNS**, page 13.*

INITIAL CODES STYLE/FONT

*To set the initial codes style, see **Default Document Style**, page 23. To set the initial font, see **Font**, page 31.*

JUSTIFICATION

> *NOTES: Text is left justified by default.*
>
> *To show the Format toolbar, click **View**, **Toolbars**. Select **Format** and click **OK**.*

1. Select paragraph(s) to justify.

   OR

   Place cursor where justification is to begin.

continued...

2. Click **Justification** ▤ to open drop-down menu.

   *NOTE: The **Justification** toolbar button varies in appearance because it always displays the current justification setting.*

3. Select desired justification:

   - ▤ **Left**... [Ctrl]+[L]
   - ▤ **Center** .... [Ctrl]+[E]
   - ▤ **Right** .... [Ctrl]+[R]
   - ▤ **Full**.. [Ctrl]+[J]
   - ▤ **All**

   *NOTE: The **All** justification option aligns all lines, including the last line in the paragraph.*

KEEP TEXT TOGETHER

Gives you access to three features: Widow/Orphan, Block protect, and Conditional end of page.

***Widow/Orphan** prevents single lines at the beginning (widow) or end (orphan) of a paragraph from appearing at the bottom or top of a page. By default, Widow/Orphan control is enabled.*

***Block protect** keeps selected text together, not allowing it to be divided between two pages. This feature is often used to keep a table together, for example.*

***Conditional end of page**, which is often used to keep a heading with the first lines of the first paragraph after the heading. Keeps a specified number of lines together on a page.*

1. Place cursor where you want to keep a specific number of lines together.

   OR

   Select text to keep on same page.

continued...

KEEP TEXT TOGETHER (CONTINUED)

2. Click **Fo**r**mat**, **K**eep Text Together ..... Alt + R , K

3. Click **P**revent the first .... P
   **and last lines of paragraphs from being separated
   across pages** check box (widow/orphan option).

   OR

   Click **K**eep selected text together................... K
   on same page check box (block protect option).

   OR

   a. Click **N**umber of lines .... N
      to keep together check box
      (conditional end of page option).

   b. Type number of lines.............................*number*
      to keep together.

4. Click ⟨ OK ⟩ .... ↵

LABELS

*When you create labels in WordPerfect, you have logical pages and
physical pages. Each label is a **logical page**. Each page of labels is
a **physical page**. So, for example, you may have thirty labels
(logical pages) on one page of labels (physical page).*

Label definitions *contain all the predefined information you need to
format pages of labels: it defines the printer type, label size, and so
forth. Label definitions are stored in **label files**.*

*After setting up your document with a label definition, you can
merge from a data file to create labels. See **MERGE**, page 69.*

View Labels

*You can type labels in any view. In Draft view, labels are separated
with a dotted line and do not appear the way they will print. To see
how labels will print, use Page view (**Alt+F5**) or Two Pages view
(**V**iew, **Two** Pages).*

WordPerfect 61

Select Label Definition

1. Place cursor on page where labels are to begin.

2. Click **Format**, **Labels**......................`Alt`+`R`, `B`

3. Click desired **List labels for** option (displays label definitions for type of paper selected):

   - **Laser printed** ....`R`
     lists label definitions for single sheets

   - **Tractor-fed** ....`T`
     lists label definitions for continuous pages (e.g., dot-matrix printers).

   - **Both** ....`B`
     lists label definitions for both laser and tractor-fed printers.

4. Select desired **Labels** definition ...`Alt`+`L`, `↑` `↓`

5. Click `Select` ....`↵`

Enter Text in Labels

TO:	PRESS:
Insert address from address book	See **Address Book**, page 1.
Merge from a file containing names and addresses	See **Merge**, page 69.
End text on current label and move to next label	`Ctrl`+`↵`
End line of text within label	`↵`
Move to next label	`Alt`+`Page Up`
Move to previous label	`Alt`+`Page Down`

Create/Edit Label Definition

1. Click **Fo_r_mat**, **La_b_els** .... `Alt`+`R`, `B`

2. Click [_C_reate...] .... `Alt`+`C`

   OR

   Select definition and click [_E_dit...] .... `Alt`+`E`

3. Set options as desired.

4. Click [OK] twice .... `↵`, `↵`
   if necessary.

Discontinue Labels

1. Click **Fo_r_mat**, **La_b_els** .... `Alt`+`R`, `B`

2. Click [_O_ff] .... `Alt`+`O`

   NOTE: *When you turn labels off before the end of*
   a page, WordPerfect completes the rest of
   the page with blank labels.

Print Specific Pages of Labels

1. Click **Print** 🖶 .... `Ctrl`+`P`

2. Click **_M_ultiple Pages** .... `M`

3. Click [Multiple Pages] .... `Ctrl`+`Tab`

4. Type page numbers .... `Alt`+`P`, *number(s)*
   of labels to print in **Page(s)/label(s)** text box.

   EXAMPLE: *1,3-4,7*

5. Click [Print] .... `↵`

*(See **Print**, page 89, for more information.)*

LINE NUMBERING

Print line numbers using your choice of numbering formats.

1. Place cursor where numbering is to begin.

   > *NOTE:* Numbering begins on the first line of the
   > paragraph containing the cursor.

2. Click **Fo<u>r</u>mat**, **<u>L</u>ine** .... `Alt`+`R`, `L`

3. Click **<u>N</u>umbering**... `N`

4. Click **Turn line numbering <u>o</u>n** check box .... `O`

5. Select any desired options.

6. Click `OK` .... `◄┘`

   > *NOTES:* Depending on the options you choose for
   > the **Position of numbers**, you may not be
   > able to see the change on the screen. The
   > line numbers will appear, however, when
   > you print the document.
   >
   > To turn line numbers off, repeat the steps
   > above, placing the cursor where numbering
   > is to end in step 1, and deselecting the
   > **Turn line numbering <u>o</u>n** check box in
   > step 4.

LINE SPACING

Set Fixed Line Height

***Line height** is the measurement from the top of a line
of text to the top of the next line of text.*

1. Place cursor where change will begin.

   OR
   Select paragraph(s) to change.

2. Click **Fo<u>r</u>mat**, **<u>L</u>ine** .... `Alt`+`R`, `L`

continued...

SET FIXED LINE HEIGHT (CONTINUED)

3. Click **H**eight.. `H`

4. Click **F**ixed radio button .... `F`

5. Select **F**ixed line height measurement..... ..... `Tab`
   using increment arrows (also known as *spin
   buttons*) 🔼 , or type desired amount in text box.

6. Click `  OK  ` .... `↵`

   NOTE: *To return to automatic line height, click the*
               Automatic *radio button in step 4.*

Change Line Spacing

*Changes line spacing based on a percentage of the current line
height (e.g., 1.5 times the current line height).*

1. Place cursor where change will begin.

   OR

   Select paragraph(s) to change.

2. Click **Fo**rmat, **L**ine........................... `Alt`+`R`,`L`

3. Click **S**pacing .... `S`

4. Select line **S**pacing measurement using increment
   arrows (also known as *spin buttons*) 🔼 , or type
   amount by which you want to multiply the current
   line height.

   NOTE: **Line height** *is measured from the top of a
               line to the top of the next line. A number
               smaller than 1 reduces space (e.g., .09
               reduces space while 1.5 adds space).*

5. Click `  OK  ` .... `↵`

WordPerfect 65

MACROS

NOTE: To run a macro from a hyperlink, see
Create Hyperlink on page 50.

Record Macro

CAUTION: When recording a macro, WordPerfect
can include mouse actions such as
selecting a command from a menu,
however. Do not use the mouse to
position the cursor; use the keys if
you wish to record cursor movements
in the macro.

1. Click **Tools, Macro, Record** .... `Ctrl`+`F10`

2. Type macro **File name**.............................. *filename*

3. Click [Record].. `↵`

The Macro feature bar displays:

| ■ | ○ | ▶ | ‖ | Dialog Editor... | Commands... | Save & Compile | Codes... | Options ▾ |

4. Use WordPerfect to record desired commands.

   To pause/resume recording:

   Click Macro feature bar `‖` .... `Alt`+`T`, `M`, `U`

   To stop recording:

   Click Macro feature bar `■` .... `Ctrl`+`F10`

Play Back Macro

1. Place cursor where macro is to begin.

2. Press **Alt+F10**...................................... `Alt`+`F10`

3. Double-click macro to play.

   To pause/resume macro:

   Click Macro feature bar `‖` ... `Alt`+`T`, `M`, `U`

Play Back Recently Used Macro

> *NOTE:*   *The last macros you recorded or played are listed on the **Tools**, **Macro** menu.*

1. Place cursor where macro is to begin.

2. Click **T**ools, **M**acro .... `Alt`+`T`,`M`

3. Click macro to play (at bottom of drop-down menu), or type number shown next to desired macro.

Record QuickMacro

*A **QuickMacro** is one that you do not save. For example, if you are repeating the same format in a document, record a QuickMacro to do the formatting for you. When you exit WordPerfect, the QuickMacro is deleted. You can only have one QuickMacro in a document at a time.*

1. Click **T**ools, Tem**p**late Macro .... `Alt`+`T`,`P`

2. Click **R**ecord .... `R`

   > *NOTE:*   *Do not enter a macro name.*

3. Click ⟨ Record ⟩ .... `↵`

4. Use WordPerfect to record desired commands.

5. Click Macro feature bar ⟨■⟩ ..... `Alt`+`T`,`P`,`R` to stop recording.

Play Back QuickMacro

1. Click **T**ools, Tem**p**late Macro .... `Alt`+`T`,`P`

2. Click **P**lay .... `P`

3. Click ⟨ Play ⟩ .... `↵`

MAKE IT FIT EXPERT

Make the current document fit a certain number of pages.
*Use **Make It Fit** to make a long document shorter or a*
short document longer.

1. Click **Format, Make It Fit** .... Alt + R , I

Make It Fit ? X

Document page count
Current number of pages: 6
Desired number of pages: 5

[Make It Fit]
[Cancel]
[Help]

Items to adjust
☐ Left margin   ☑ Font size
☐ Right margin   ☑ Line spacing
☐ Top margin
☐ Bottom margin

When Make It Fit has finished, you can press Ctrl+Z or click
the Undo button to return the document to its original state.

MAKE IT FIT DIALOG BOX

2. Type or select **Desired number of pages**... *number*

3. Select desired **Items to adjust** check box option.

4. Click [Make It Fit] .... Alt + M

MARGINS

Change Left/Right Margins Using Ruler

*NOTE: To show ruler, press **Shift+Alt+F3**.*

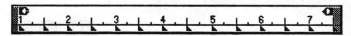

1. Place cursor where new margins will start.

   OR

   Select paragraph(s) to format.

2. Drag ▣ (margin marker) to new position.

The margin measurement displays as you move the marker.

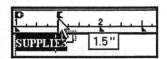

Change Any Margin Using Dialog Box

1. Place cursor where new margins will start.

   OR

   Select paragraph(s) to format.

2. Click **Fo_r_mat**, **M_a_rgins** .... Ctrl + F8

3. Type or select **Left**, **Right**, **Top**, and/or **Bottom** margin setting(s) for margin(s) to change.

   NOTES: Zero (0) is the edge of the page.

   When typing a measurement, you can type a fraction. WordPerfect converts fractions to decimals.

4. Click ⎣ OK ⎦ .... ↵

MERGE

Form Documents and Data Files

*Merging combines a form document with a series of records from a data source. The **data source** contains information such as names and addresses that are merged into the form document. The data source may be a file especially created for merging purposes, or it may be an address book. The Merge procedure is controlled by the form file.*

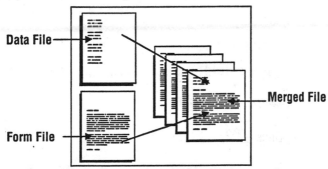

Data File

Merged File

Form File

For example, you might merge to create envelopes or form letters for everyone in a particular address book.

Data Files

*You can create two different types of data files—text or table. In any **data file**, information is divided into records and fields. For example, each record might contain a name, title, and address for one person. Therefore, **Name**, **Title**, and **Address** are the three fields in the record.*

*In a **data text file**, a special ENDFIELD command and a hard return ends each field. A special ENDRECORD command and a hard page break ends each record. Follow the **Create New Data File** procedure on page 70.*

*In a **data table file**, the first row contains field names. Then, each cell is a field and each row is a record.*

*You can use an address book as a data file. Follow the **Create Form Document** procedure on page 74.*

Create New Data File

1. Press **Shift+F9** .... `Shift` + `F9`

2. Click `Create Data ...` .... `↵`

3. Click **New document window** .... `N`
   if necessary.

4. Click `OK` .... `↵`
   if necessary.

5. Add fields to data file:

   a. **Name a field** .... *field name*

   EXAMPLE: *first name*

   b. Click `Add` .... `↵`

   c. Repeat steps a and b until all fields are added.

   d. Click `OK` .... `↵`
      when finished adding fields.

*The **Quick Data Entry** dialog box displays the data file fields
that you added. Use the dialog box to add records to the data
file.*

6. Enter record data:

   a. Type data for field .... *text*

   b. Press **Enter** or **Tab** .... `↵` or `Tab`
      to move to next field.

   NOTE: *Pressing **Enter** at the last field creates
               a new record.*

   c. Repeat steps a and b until all records are added.

continued.

WordPerfect 71

7. Save data file:

   a. Click `Close` .... `Alt`+`C`

   b. Click `Yes` .... `↵`
      to save the changes to (hard) disk.

   c. Type **File name** .... *filename*

   d. Click `Save` .... `↵`

Edit Field Names

Adds, deletes, and replaces field names.

1. Create or open data file.

   *NOTE: The Merge feature bar automatically
            displays when you open a data file.*

2. Click `Quick Entry...` .... `Shift`+`Alt`+`Q`

3. Click `Field Names...` .... `Alt`+`A`

   To add field name(s):

   a. Click field name .... `Alt`+`U`, `↑` `↓`
      before which you wish
      to add field name(s).

   b. Type new field name .... `Alt`+`F`, *field name*
      over selected **Field name**.

   c. Click `Add Before` .... `Alt`+`B`

   To delete field name(s):

   a. Click field name .... `Alt`+`U`, `↑` `↓`
      to delete.

   b. Click `Delete` .... `Alt`+`D`

   c. Click `OK` .... `↵`

continued...

EDIT FIELD NAMES (CONTINUED)

To replace field name(s):

a. Click field name .... `Alt`+`U`, `↑` `↓`

b. Edit **F**ield name as desired .... `Alt`+`F`

c. Click [**R**eplace] .... `Alt`+`R`

d. Click [OK] .... `↵`

4. Click [OK] .... `↵`

5. Click [**C**lose] .... `Alt`+`C`

6. Click [**Y**es] .... `↵`
   to save the changes (hard) disk.

Use Existing Data File

1. Open the data file.

2. Press **Shift+F9** to display .. .. `Shift`+`F9`
   Merge dialog box.

3. Click [Create **D**ata ...] .... `↵`

4. Click **U**se file in active window .... `U`
   radio button.

5. Click [OK] .... `↵`

Edit Data File

1. Create or open data file.

   NOTE: *The Merge feature bar automatically*
           displays when you open a data file.

2. Click [**Q**uick Entry...] .... `Shift`+`Alt`+`Q`

continued...

WordPerfect 73

To find record:

a. Click `Find...` .... `Alt`+`I`

b. Type field data to find................................. *text*

c. Click `Find Next` .... `↵`

To delete record:

a. Display record.

b. Click `Delete Record` .... `Alt`+`D`

CAUTION: *Deletion is not confirmed, but may be restored. (See* **Undo***, page 131.)*

To create new record:

Click `New Record` .... `Alt`+`R`

3. Click `Close` .... `Esc`

4. Click `Yes` .... `↵`
to save changes to (hard) disk.

Sort Data File

Merged documents are created in the order in which they appear in the data file. If, for example, you want them to print in zip code order, sort the data file by zip code before merging.

1. Create or open data file.

2. Click `Options ▼` .... `Shift`+`Alt`+`O`

3. Click **Sort** .... `S`

4. Select option as desired.

5. Click `Sort` .... `↵`

Create Form Document

1. Press **Shift+F9** .... Shift + F9

2. Click [Create Document...] C

3. Click **Use file in active window** .... U
   radio button.

   OR

   Click **New document window** .... N
   radio button.

4. Click [OK] .... ↵

5. Specify data file as follows:

   - **Associate a data file** — Select data file created using **Create New Data File** procedure.

   - **Associate an address book** — Select address book to use.

   - **Associate an ODBC Data Source** — ODBC data sources stored on network.

   - **No association** — Use if you have not yet created a data file.

6. Click [OK] .... ↵

continued...

7. Format and type document. Take special care to enter punctuation and spacing between fields.

   NOTE: There may be cases where you will need to add punctuation and spacing to the data file rather than the form file. Always check your merged document before printing.

   To add a field from the data file:

   a. Click `Insert Field...` .... `Shift`+`Alt`+`I`

   b. Select field name............................. `↑` `↓`

   c. Click `Insert` .... `Alt`+`I`

8. Repeat step 7 until form document is complete.

   *NOTE: To switch to associated data file, click the **Data Source** button. Then, click **Data File** on the pop-up menu.*

9. Click `Close` .... `Esc`
   in **Insert Field Name or Number** dialog box.

10. Save the form document:

    a. Press **Ctrl+S**.................................... `Ctrl`+`S`

    b. Type **File name**................................... *filename*

    c. Click `Save` .... `↵`

Perform Merge

—WITH MERGE FEATURE BAR ACTIVE—

1. Click [Merge...] .... Shift + Alt + M

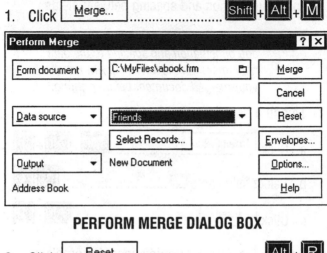

PERFORM MERGE DIALOG BOX

2. Click [Reset] .... Alt + R
   to clear all options, if desired.

3. Select **Form document** F4
   option from pop–up list.

4. Select or type filename .... *filename*, ↑ ↓ ⏎

5. Select **Data source** .... Alt + D, F4, ↑ ↓
   option from pop-up list.

   OR

   Click **None** .... N
   if performing keyboard merge.

6. Select desired .... Alt + U, F4, ↑ ↓ ⏎
   Output file from pop–up list.

   *NOTE: The **output file** is the file or printer in which you
   will save or print the merged document(s).*

continued..

WordPerfect 77

7. Follow **Select Records to Merge**, below, to use a subset of the records in the data source, if desired.

   NOTE: *For example, you might want to create form letters for only residents in a particular state.*

8. Select desired [**Options...**] .... `Alt`+`O`, `↵` from **Perform Merge Options** dialog box.

9. Click [**Merge**] .... `Alt`+`M`

Select Records to Merge

Select a subset of the records in the data source to use for the merge.

1. Complete steps 1–6, **Perform Merge**, above.

2. Click [**Select Records...**] .... `Alt`+`S`, `↵`

   NOTE: *If the data source is an address book, you can select an address list or press **Ctrl** and click to select individual records.*

3. Click **Mark records** .... `Alt`+`A` radio button.

   NOTE: *You can also enter conditions for each field. Click **Specify conditions** radio button and click the **Help** or **Example** button. You can also right-click an option to see a description.*

   *For example, using the **Specify conditions** radio button option, you could select all records for a particular city or zip code using conditions.*

continued...

SELECT RECORDS TO MERGE (CONTINUED)

To display particular records in the Record list (box):

a. Type range .... Alt+D, *number,* Tab, *number* of records to display in the **Display records from** and **to** text boxes.

b. Select field.............. Alt + F, F4, ↑, ↓, ⏎ from **First field to display** list, if desired.

NOTE: Use the step above to hide fields in the Record list so that you can locate specific records. For example, you might want to include only those records in a particular city. If you sorted records by city (see Sort Data File procedure), you can quickly show all records for a single city by hiding fields that appear before the City field.

c. Click | Update Record List | .... Alt+U to display selected records in **Record list**.

The records will be displayed in the Record list.

4. Click records .... Alt+L, ↑, ↓ to merge in the **Records list**.

   OR

   Click | Mark All Records in List | .... Alt+M

5. Click | OK | .... ⏎

6. Click | Merge | .... ⏎

OPEN DOCUMENT

Open Recently Used Document

1. Click **File**.. .... `Alt`+`F`

2. Click file to open .... *number*

Open Any Document

1. Click **Open** 📇 .... `Ctrl`+`O`

2. Double-click file to open.

> *NOTE:* *WordPerfect displays files in the last directory that you used in the current session or the default document folder. (See **Default Document Folder**, page 22.)*

OUTLINE

Show Outline Toolbar

1. Click **View**, **Toolbars**...................... `Alt`+`V`, `T`

2. Click to select **Outline Tools** check box from **Available toolbars** list.

The Outline toolbar displays:

3. Click `OK` ....

Create Outline Using Heading Styles

Apply Heading styles to paragraphs to indicate headings and subheadings.

> *NOTE:* *Use WordPerfect's built-in heading styles; for example, apply the Heading 1 style to the title, Heading 2 to the next heading level, etc. This creates outline levels. You can edit Heading style formatting if desired. Use the Outline toolbar to promote/demote headings, view headings only, etc.*

Create Numbered Automatic Outline

1. Position cursor where outline will begin.

2. Click **I**nsert .... `Alt`+`I`

3. Click **Outline/Bullets & Numbering** .... `N`

4. Click `Numbers` .... `Ctrl`+`Tab`

5. Click to select **Start new outline or list** .... `S`
   radio button if not already selected.

6. Click to select desired outline style.

7. Click `OK` .... `⏎`

8. Type text .... *text*

9. Press **Enter** .... `⏎`

The new paragraph is assigned an outline level (e.g., Level 1, Level 2).

10. Repeat steps 8 and 9, if desired, to type paragraph using current outline level.

   OR

   Click **Demote** `→-` .... `Tab`
   to change paragraph outline
   level to next lower level.

   OR

   Click **Promote** `←-` .... `Shift`+`Tab`
   to change paragraph outline
   level to next higher level.

11. Repeat steps 8-10 until outline is complete.

End Automatic Outline

Use this procedure to discontinue outlining so that you can enter text without automatically applying outline levels. (You can later resume automatic outlining if you wish.) Text that you type after ending the outline is considered body text.

1. Press **Enter**.. ⏎
   in last paragraph to apply
   bullets or numbers.

2. Press **Backspace** .... Backspace

Resume Automatic Outline

Continues numbering from the next outline number/letter from where you stopped the automatic outline.

1. Position cursor where outline will restart.

2. Click **Insert** .... Alt + I

3. Click **Outline/Bullets & Numbering** .... N

4. Click Numbers .... Ctrl + Tab

5. Click to select **Resume outline or list**.............. R
   radio button if not already selected.

6. Click OK .... ⏎

   *NOTE: Type text as described in **Create Numbered Automatic Outline**, page 80, steps 8-11.*

Renumber Outline

Renumber an outline starting from the cursor position or change the starting number when you type new text.

—WITH OUTLINE TOOLBAR ACTIVE—

1. Place cursor in paragraph where renumbering will start.

2. Click **Set Paragraph Number** 🔲

3. Type number to start with ....*start number* in **Paragraph <u>n</u>umber** text box.

4. Click ⬚ OK ⬚ .... ⏎

PAGE BREAK

Insert Hard Page Break

1. Place cursor where new page is to begin.

2. Press **Ctrl+Enter**.................................. `Ctrl` + ⏎

   OR

   Press **Ctrl+Shift+Enter** .... `Ctrl` + `Shift` + ⏎
   to insert in columns.

   NOTE: ***Ctrl+Enter*** *creates a column break in multiple columns.*

In Draft view, a double horizontal line marks the page break.

Delete Page Break

1. Place cursor directly beneath page break.

2. Press **Backspace**...................................... `Backspace`

WordPerfect

PAGE NUMBERING

Number Pages

You can also add page numbers to headers and footers.
*See **Headers/Footers** on page 47.*

1. Place cursor where numbering is to begin.

2. Click **For**mat, **Page** .... Alt + R , P

3. Click **Numbering** .... N

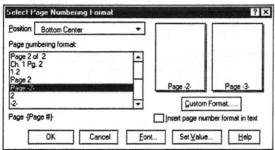

SELECT PAGE NUMBERING FORMAT DIALOG BOX

4. Select desired location .... F4 , ↑ , ↓ , ↵
   in **Position** pop–up list.

Selected page number position and format appear in
sample at right side of dialog box.

5. Select desired format .... Alt + N , ↑ ↓
   in **Page numbering format** list box.

6. Click ⬜ OK .... ↵

Include Chapter, Volume, and
Secondary Page Numbers

1. Place cursor where numbering is to begin.

2. Click **For**mat, **Page** .... Alt + R , P

continued…

INCLUDE CHAPTER, VOLUME, SECONDARY PAGE NUMBERS (CONTINUED)

3. Click **Numbering** .... N

4. Click Custom Format... .... Alt + C

Custom Page Numbering   ? X

Select a number style and insert it in the custom format.

Page:	Total pgs:	Chapter:	Volume:	Secondary pg:
1,2,3,...	1,2,3...	1,2,3,...	1,2,3,...	1,2,3,...
a,b,c,...	a,b,c,...	a,b,c,...	a,b,c,...	a,b,c,...
A,B,C,...	A,B,C,...	A,B,C,...	A,B,C,...	A,B,C,...
i,ii,iii,...	i,ii,iii,...	i,ii,iii,...	i,ii,iii,...	i,ii,iii,...
I,II,III,...	I,II,III,...	I,II,III,...	I,II,III,...	I,II,III,...

Insert in format

Custom page numbering format (numbering codes with text):

Chapter [Chpt #]--Page [Page #] of [Tot Pages #]

Chapter 1--Page 2 of 2

OK   Cancel   Help

CUSTOM PAGE NUMBERING DIALOG BOX

---

5. Type text to appear before number in **Custom page numbering format** (numbering codes with text) text box, if desired.

6. Click number(s) to insert (from **Page**, **Total Pgs**, **Chapter**, **Volume**, and/or **Secondary pg** lists).

7. Click Insert in format .... Alt + I

8. Repeat steps 5-7 as desired to create custom format.

   *NOTE: An example of the format that you have created appears directly under the **Custom page numbering format** text box.*

9. Click   OK   .... ↵

10. Click   OK

Increase/Decrease Numbers

1. Place cursor where number change is to begin.

2. Click **For̲mat**, **P̲age** .... **Alt**+**R**, **P**

3. Click **N̲umbering** .... **N**

4. Click **Set V̲alue...** .... **Alt**+**V**

Values	? X
Page Chapter Volume Secondary	

S̲et page number: **1** ⬍

◉ Al̲ways keep number the same.
○ L̲et number change as pages are added or deleted.

| OK | Cancel | A̲pply | H̲elp |

VALUES DIALOG BOX, PAGE TAB

5. Click **Page** .... **Ctrl**+**Tab**
   if not already selected.

6. Type interval number .... *number*
   by which you would like to increase
   or decrease **S̲et page number**.

7. Select **Al̲ways keep number the same** .... **Alt**+**W**

   OR

   Select **L̲et number change as** .... **Alt**+**L**
   pages are added or deleted.

8. Click **OK** twice .... **↵**, **↵**

Change Font/Appearance of Numbers

1. Place cursor where number change is to begin.

2. Click **Fo_r_mat**, **_P_age**.......................... `Alt`+`R`, `P`

3. Click **_N_umbering** .... `N`

4. Click `Font...` ....`Alt`+`F`

5. Set format option(s).

6. Click `OK` twice................. ....`↵`, `↵`

Suppress Page Number for Current Page

1. Place cursor where number suppression is to begin.

2. Click **Fo_r_mat**, **_P_age**............ .... `Alt`+`R`, `P`

3. Click **_S_uppress** .... `U`

4. Click to select **_P_age numbering** check box...... `P`

5. Click `OK` .... `↵`

Force Odd, Even, or New Page

1. Place cursor on page to force.

2. Click **Fo_r_mat**, **_P_age**............... .... `Alt`+`R`, `P`

3. Click **_F_orce Page** .... `F`

4. Select desired **Force Page** radio button option.

5. Click `OK` .... `↵`

PAPER SIZE

Select Paper Definition

1. Place cursor where changes are to begin.
2. Click **File**, **Page Setup** .... Alt + F , G
3. Click [Size] .... Ctrl + Tab
   if not already selected.
4. Select desired **Page information** .... ↑ ↓
5. Click [OK] .... ↵

PARAGRAPH FORMAT

Change Format Options

Set first-line indent, space between paragraphs, and left and right margin indents.

1. Place cursor where changes are to begin.

   OR

   Select paragraphs to format.
2. Click **Format**, **Paragraph** .... Alt + R , A
3. Click **Format** .... F

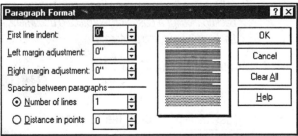

PARAGRAPH FORMAT DIALOG BOX

4. Select desired measurements and options.
5. Click [OK] .... ↵

PASSWORD

Save File with Password

—IN SAVE AS DIALOG BOX—

1. Select file to save with password, if different from open file.

2. Click to select **Password Protect**............ Alt + P check box.

3. Click [**Save**] .... ↵

4. Click [**Yes**] .... ↵
to verify replacing file with password–protected file, if necessary.

5. **Type Password for Document**................*password*

6. Select desired **Protection Options**.

7. Click [**OK**] .... ↵

8. **Retype Password to Confirm** ....*password*

9. Click [**OK**] .... ↵

> *NOTE: The Password feature cannot be used with all files or applications. Saving a password–protected file in a non–WordPerfect format or in WordPerfect 4.2 format will remove the password. If you automatically save backup files for a password–protected document, the backup files are also protected.*

Open Password–Protected File

1. Click **File**, **Open**.............................. Ctrl + O

2. Select password–protected file to open.

3. Click [**Open**] .... ↵

4. Type file's password...............................*password*

5. Click [**OK**] .... ↵

Remove Password from File

1. Open password–protected file.

2. Click **File, Save As**.......................... `Alt`+`F`, `A`

3. Click **Password protect** to deselect........ `Alt`+`P`

4. Click | Save | .... `↵`

5. Click | Yes | .... `↵`
   at the **Error** box to confirm.

PRINT

Select Printer

1. Click **File, Print**.............................. `Ctrl`+`P`

2. Click | Print | .... `Ctrl`+`Tab`
   if necessary.

3. Select **Current**........... `Alt`+`U`, `F4`, `↑` `↓`, `↵`
   printer.

   NOTE: Lists printers installed through Windows.

   To set printer properties:

   a. Click | Properties | .... `Alt`+`O`

   b. Set options as desired.

   c. Click | OK | .... `↵`

   To set printer details:

   a. Click | Details | .... `Ctrl`+`Tab`

   b. Set options as desired.

   *NOTE: The higher the resolution, the more system
   resources (such as memory and disk
   space) are required to print the document.*

4. Click | Close | .... `Alt`+`C`

Print Document

To print selected text only:

Select text to print.

To print current page only:

Position cursor in page to print.

1. Click **Print** 🖨 .... `Ctrl` + `P`

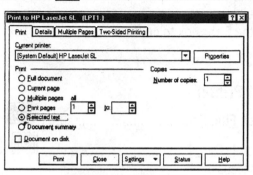

PRINT DIALOG BOX

2. Select desired **Print** option(s).

> *NOTES:*   *The **Selected text** radio button option is available only if text has been selected.*
>
> *The **Document summary** radio button option is available only if you have created a document summary.*
>
> *If the desired printer is not the current printer, see **Printers**, page 91.*

To print multiple copies:

a. Click **Number of copies** .... `Alt` + `N`

b. Type or select number .... *number* of copies to print.

c. Click **Collate copies** .... `Alt` + `A`/`G`
or **Group copies** radio button to specify order in which pages print.

continued..

To print only desired pages:

a. Click **Multiple pages** to print certain sections.

b. Click [Multiple Pages] .... `Ctrl` + `Tab`
to specify pages to print.

OR

a. Click **Print pages** .... `Alt` + `P`

b. Enter or select first page .... `Tab`, *number*
to print.

c. Enter or select last page .... `Tab`, *number*
to print.

3. Click [Print] .... `↵`

NOTE: *To cancel print job, click **Print** button on*
*toolbar; or, in the printer **Status** dialog box,*
*click **Printer**, **Cancel Print Job** from the*
menu.

PRINTERS

Printer Setup

1. Click **Print** 🖨 .... `Ctrl` + `P`

2. Click [Print] .... `Ctrl` + `Tab`

3. Select printer .... `Alt` + `U`, `F4`, `↑`, `↓`
from **Current printer** list.

NOTE: *The **Current printer** drop-down list displays*
printers installed through Windows.

4. Click [Properties] .... `Alt` + `O`

5. Set options as desired.

continued...

PRINTER SETUP (CONTINUED)

6. Click [OK] .... [↵]

To set printer details:

a. Click [Details] .... [Ctrl]+[Tab]

b. Set options as desired.

To make new printer current printer:

a. Select desired printer .... [F4], [↑][↓]

b. Click [Close] .... [Alt]+[C]

Add Printer

1. Click **Print** 🖶 .... [Ctrl]+[P]

2. Click [Details] ....[Ctrl]+[Tab]

3. Click [Add Printer] .... [Alt]+[A]

4. Follow **Add Printer Wizard** prompts.

QUICKCORRECT

Automatically corrects spelling errors, capitalization mistakes, and other common typing errors as you type. Also expands abbreviations.

Add an Abbreviation for a Word

Use this procedure to specify which corrections QuickCorrect will make as you type and to add abbreviations that QuickCorrect will automatically expand.

1. Click **Tools**, **QuickCorrect**............... [Alt]+[T], [Q]

2. Type abbreviation/word .... *abbreviation*
   to **Replace** in text box.

continued...

3. Type word(s) .... `Tab`, *word(s)*
   to replace in **With** text box.

   *NOTE: For example, you could enter **u** or **univ** for*
   *__university__ and **mgt** for __management__.*

4. Click [**A**dd Entry] .... `Alt`+`A`

5. Repeat steps 1–4 to add additional abbreviations.

   NOTE: QuickCorrect must be enabled for it to
   automatically expand abbreviations as you
   *type. The **R**eplace words as you type*
   check box should be marked (the default).

6. Press **Esc** ....:.............. `Esc`
   to exit **QuickCorrect** dialog box.

Add Abbreviation for Phrase or Paragraph(s)

1. Select text in document.

2. Click **T**ools, **Quick**W**ords .... `Alt`+`T`,`W`

3. Type abbreviation... *text*

4. Click [**A**dd Entry] .... `Alt`+`A`

   NOTE: QuickCorrect must be enabled for it to
   automatically expand abbreviations as
   *you type. The **Expand QuickWords as***
   ***you type them** check box must be marked*
   (the default).

Set Automatic Formatting Options

1. Click **Tools**, **QuickCorrect**............... `Alt`+`T`,`Q`

2. Click `Format-As-You-Go` .... `Ctrl`+`Tab`

3. Set options as desired.

4. Click `OK` .... `↵`

QUICKFORMAT

Copy Format of Paragraph

*QuickFormat creates and applies paragraph styles (called QuickFormat1, QuickFormat2, etc.) from copied paragraph formatting. If you change any of the style elements in a QuickFormat paragraph, the same formatting change is applied to all other paragraphs that you copied the formatting to. If you wish to prevent this, complete the **Disable QuickFormat Updates** procedure, below.*

1. Place cursor in paragraph containing format to copy.

2. Click **QuickFormat** .... `Alt`+`R`,`Q`

3. Click **Headings** radio button .... `E`
   if not selected.

4. Click `OK` .... `↵`

5. Drag paint–roller cursor over text to format.

6. Repeat step 5 to format more paragraphs, if desired.

7. Click **QuickFormat** .... `Alt`+`R`,`Q`
   to end.

Disable QuickFormat Updates

Use this procedure if you do not want future formatting changes applied to paragraphs formatted using QuickFormat.

1. Click in paragraph that has QuickFormat style.

2. Click **QuickFormat** `[✎]` .... `Alt`+`R`,`Q`

3. Click `Discontinue` .... `D`

4. Click **Current heading** .... `C`
   to discontinue updating the current
   paragraph with changes.

   OR

   Click **All associated headings** .... `A`
   to prevent updating all paragraphs
   with the QuickFormat style.

5. Click `OK` .... `↵`

Copy Format of Text

1. Select formatted text.

2. Click **QuickFormat** `[✎]` .... `Alt`+`R`,`Q`

3. Click **Selected characters** radio button............ `S`
   if not selected.

4. Drag paintbrush cursor across characters
   to format.

5. Repeat step 4, as desired, to copy formatting
   to other text.

6. Click **QuickFormat** `[✎]` .... `Alt`+`R`,`Q`
   to end.

REVEAL CODES

1. Press **Alt+F3** ....

   NOTE: *To make Reveal Codes window smaller/larger, drag window dividing line.*

2. Move through Reveal Codes window as desired.

   NOTE: *You can move the cursor in the Reveal Codes window the same way you move through a document.*

3. Repeat step 1 to hide Reveal Codes window.

   NOTE: *To show/hide space, hard return, tab, and indent symbols in the document itself, press **Ctrl+Shift+F3**.*

Delete Codes

Use **Backspace/Delete** keys .... Backspace or Delete

OR

Drag code out of Reveal Codes window.

   NOTE: *Some codes consist of two codes—one to turn on formatting and the next to turn it off. For example, bold text consists of two Bold codes—one before the boldface text and one after. Deleting one Bold code deletes both codes and thus the formatting itself.*

Edit a Code

For example, to change the font, double-click a font code (such as Bold) to open the Font dialog box. Double-click a paragraph style code to open the Styles Editor dialog box.

1. Double–click the code.
2. Edit in dialog box as desired.

Find and Replace Codes

*Locates and replaces codes quickly. (See **Find**, page 27, for more information.)*

RULER

Format Using the Ruler

- **Ruler** Appearance varies, depending on the location of the cursor. Shows formatting, such as paragraph indents and tab stop settings at the cursor position.

- **Document Ruler** You can drag margin markers to change the left and right margins, drag tab markers to move tabs, and drag the paragraph indent marker to adjust indents.

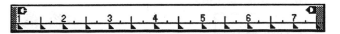

- **Column Ruler** For column text, drag margin markers to reposition column margins. You can also drag tab markers, margin markers, and paragraph indent markers.

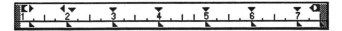

- **Table Ruler** For tables, you can drag margin markers to change left and right table margins. You can also drag table column markers to change column positions in the table.

Display/Hide Ruler

Press **Alt+Shift+F3** .... `Alt`+`Shift`+`F3`

> *NOTE: Repeat the step above to hide the ruler.*

Change Ruler Settings

1. Click **Tools**, **Settings** .... `Alt`+`T`, `N`

2. Double-click Display .... `↵`

   ### To set ruler unit of measurement:

   a. Click `Document` .... `Ctrl`+`Tab`
      if necessary.

   b. Select **Application** ..... `Alt`+`Y`, `F4`, `↑`, `↓`, `↵`
      Bar/Ruler display setting.

   ### To set ruler gridlines:

   a. Click `Ruler` .... `Ctrl`+`Tab`

   b. Select desired option(s).

   > *NOTE: The ruler grid has vertical gridlines placed
   > at 1/16" intervals.*

3. Click `OK` .... `↵`

4. Click `Close` .... `Esc`

SAVE

Save Document and Continue Working

Press **Ctrl+S** .... `Ctrl`+`S`

   If creating new document:

   a. Type **File name** .... *filename*
      in text box.

   > *NOTE: Select path to file in **Save in** drop-down list
   > box, if necessary.*

   b. Click `Save` .... `↵`

WordPerfect 99

Save Document and Exit WordPerfect

1. Press **Alt+F4** .... `Alt` + `F4`

2. Click [Yes   ] .... `↵`
   to save document changes, if necessary.

   If creating new document:

   a. Type **File name** .... *filename*
      in text box.

   *NOTE: Select path to file in **Save in** drop-down
   list box, if necessary.*

   b. Click [Save   ] .... `↵`

Save Selected Text as New Document

1. Select text to save.

2. Press **Ctrl+S** .... `Ctrl` + `S`

3. Click **Selected text** radio button .... `S`

4. Click [OK   ] .... `↵`

5. Type **File name** .... *filename*
   in text box.

   *NOTE: Specify path to file in **Save in** drop-down
   list box, if necessary.*

   EXAMPLE: c:\MyFiles\filename

6. Click [Save   ] .... `↵`

Save File with Password

*(See **Password**, page 88.)*

Backup Documents Automatically

Creates a document with the same filename as the current document with a .BK! extension.

1. Click **T**ools, Setti**n**gs .... `Alt`+`T`, `N`

2. Double-click Files .... `Tab`, `↵`

3. Click | Document | .... `Ctrl`+`Tab`

4. Type/select **B**ackup .... `Alt`+`B`, `F4` or *pathname* **folder** pathname.

   NOTE: The Backup folder is only used for timed document backups.

5. Select **T**imed document .... `Alt`+`T`, *number* **backup every *x* minutes** check box option to have WordPerfect back up documents at the specified interval.

   NOTE: Stores a copy of the document using the original filename. Saves backup copies in the Backup folder.

   AND/OR

   Select **O**riginal document backup.......... `Alt`+`O` check box option to have WordPerfect back up documents when you save.

   NOTE: Saves the backup copy in the same folder as the document is stored in. The backup copy has the same name as the original document but with a .BK! extension.

6. Click | OK | .... `↵`

7. Click | **C**lose | .... `Esc`

SELECT TEXT

Select Text Block

Drag highlight through text.

OR

1. Click starting position in text.

2. Press and hold **Shift** ....

3. Click ending position in text.

> *NOTE:*   *This procedure selects words only (you cannot **Shift** and click in the middle of a word; text to the end of the word will be selected), unless you **Turn Off Automatic Word Selection**, page 103.*

Select Word

Double–click word.

Select Sentence

Triple–click any word in sentence.

OR

Click once in left margin, next to sentence.

> *NOTE:*   *The mouse pointer must be an arrow (not an I–beam) to use the second method.*

Select Paragraph

Click any word in paragraph four times.

OR

Double–click left margin.

> *NOTE:*   *The mouse pointer must be an arrow (not an I–beam) to use the second method.*

Select Text Using Select Mode Keystrokes

1. Place cursor within text to select.

2. Press **F8** to begin Select mode .... `F8`

3. Select text using arrow keys .... `↑` `↓` `←` `→`

    *NOTE: To extend the selection to the end of the
    line, press the **End** key.*

Select Text Using Menu

1. Place cursor within text to select.

2. Click **Edit**, **Select** .... `Alt` + `E`, `L`

3. Select desired option .... `↑` `↓`, `↵`

OR

1. Right-click in left margin.

2. Select desired option .... `↑` `↓`, `↵`

Select Tabular Columns

1. Select text area from upper–left corner to
    lower–right corner of tabular column.

    *NOTE: Initial selection includes the column you
    want and part of all columns.*

2. Click **Edit**, **Select** .... `Alt` + `E`, `L`

3. Click **Tabular Column** .... `C`

    *NOTE: Final selection includes only columns
    between upper–left and lower–right
    corners of initial selection.*

WordPerfect

Select Text Using Keys

TO MOVE:	PRESS:
One character left or right	Shift + ← →
One line up or down	Shift + ↑ ↓
End of line (after codes)	Shift + End
Beginning of line (before codes)	Shift + Home
Top of screen	Shift + Page Up
Bottom of screen	Shift + Page Down
First line on previous page	Shift + Alt + Page Up
First line on next page	Shift + Alt + Page Down
One word left or right	Shift + Ctrl + ← →
One paragraph up or down	Shift + Ctrl + ↑ ↓
Beginning of document (before codes)	Shift + Ctrl + Home
End of document (after codes)	Shift + Ctrl + End

Turn Off Automatic Word Selection

WordPerfect assumes that you want to select an entire word when you select text using the mouse. Use this procedure to disable the feature so that you can select individual characters.

1. Click **T**ools, Setti**n**gs .... Alt + T , N

2. Double-click Environment .... Tab , ↵

continued...

TURN OFF AUTOMATIC WORD SELECTION (CONTINUED)

3. Click [General] .... `Ctrl`+`Tab`
   if necessary.

4. Deselect **Select whole words**.............. `Alt`+`S`
   instead of characters check box.

5. Click [OK].. `↵`

6. Click [Close]... `Esc`

SPELL CHECKER

1. Place cursor where you will start spell checking.

   OR

   Select text to check.

2. Click **Spell Check** [image].......................... `Ctrl`+`F1`

3. Click **Check** .... `Alt`+`K`, `F4`, `↑`, `↓`, `↵`
   drop–down box to specify
   part of document to check.

4. Click [Options ▼] ... `Alt`+`T`, `↑`, `↓`, `↵`, `Esc`
   and select options, if desired.

*The first word **Not Found** is shown at the bottom of
the Spell Checker tab window.*

   To replace a word by retyping it:

   a. Delete word provided .... `Alt`+`W`, `Delete`
      in **Replace with** text box.

   b. Type replacement word .... *word*

   c. Click [Replace]................................... `↵`

continued..

WordPerfect   105

To replace a word with a suggested replacement:

a. Click **Replacements** .... `Alt`+`P`, `↑` `↓`
   word from list box.

b. Click `Replace` .... `↵`

To skip the word:

Click `Skip Once` .... `Alt`+`O`
to ignore current occurrence of word.

OR

Click `Skip All` .... `Alt`+`A`
to ignore all occurrences of word.

To add the word to the dictionary:

Click `Add` .... `Alt`+`D`

5. Click `Yes` .... `↵`
   to close Spell Checker.

STYLES

Apply Style to Text

1. Place cursor where style is to begin:

   - **Paragraph style**   Place anywhere in paragraph.

   - **Character style**   Select text to format.

   - **Document style**   Place where formatting is to begin.

2. Select style from **Select Style** drop-down list
   `<None> ▼` on Font toolbar.

   OR

   a. Click **Format**, **Styles** .... `Alt`+`F8`

   b. Double-click style to apply .... `↑` `↓`, `↵`
      from list of **Available styles**.

Create Style in Style Editor

1. Click **Format**, **Styles**................................ Alt + F8

2. Click [C**r**eate...] .... Alt + R

3. Type new **Style name** in text box .... *style name*

4. Type style **Description** .... Tab ,*description*

5. Select desired style .... Tab , F4 , ↑ ↓ , ↵
   Type option.

   NOTE: *Paragraph and Character styles both have a paired and a paired–auto option. With the paired–auto option, if you format any text with the style applied, the same formatting is applied to all text formatted with that style. If you select the paired option, you must change the formatting in the style in order to change formatting for all text with the style applied.*

6. Add codes and text in **Contents** box using Styles Editor formatting options.

7. Specify **Enter** key action in character or paragraph styles:

   To continue with the same style even after pressing Enter:

   Deselect **Enter key will chain to**............. Alt + N
   check box option.

   To have Enter turn the style off, then on again:

   a. Select **Enter key will chain to**............ Alt + N
      check box option.

   b. Select **<Same Style>**............ Tab , F4 , ↑ ↓

continued...

To have Enter turn style off and leave it off:

a. Select **E**nter key will chain to .... `Alt`+`N`
   check box option.

b. Select **<None>**....................... `Tab`, `F4`, `↑` `↓`

To have Enter turn style off/turn on new style:

a. Select **E**nter key will chain to .... `Alt`+`N`
   check box option.

b. Select desired style .... `Tab`, `F4`, `↑` `↓`
   from list.

8. Click `OK` .... `↵`

9. Click `Apply` .... `↵`
   to apply style to text.

   OR

   Click `Close` .... `Esc`

Create Style from Formatted Text

Create a paragraph or character style from formatted text.

1. Place cursor in preformatted text.

2. Complete one of the following procedures:

   a. Click **Fo**rmat, **Sty**les .... `Alt`+`F8`

   b. Click `QuickStyle...` .... `Alt`+`Q`

   OR

   Select **QuickStyle...** from **Select Style** drop-down
   list `<None>  ▼` on Font toolbar.

3. Type new **Style** **n**ame in text box.......... *style name*

4. Type style **D**escription .... `Tab`, *description*

continued...

CREATE STYLE FROM FORMATTED TEXT (CONTINUED)

5. Select desired **Style type** radio button option to create a paragraph style or character style.

6. Click [OK] .... [⏎]

   If you completed Steps a and b, above:
   Click [Close] .... [Esc]
   to close **Style List** dialog box.

Delete Style in Document

DELETE INDIVIDUAL OCCURRENCES OF STYLE

Delete [Para Style: name] and/or [Para Style: name] or [Open Style: InitialStyle] in Reveal Codes window. *(See **Delete Codes**, page 96.)*

DELETE STYLE THROUGHOUT DOCUMENT

1. Click **Format, Styles**.............................. [Alt]+[F8]

2. Select style to delete in............................... [↑] [↓]
   Available styles list box.

3. Click [Options ▼] .... [Alt]+[O], [F4]

4. Click **Delete**... [D]

5. Select **Including format codes** .... [I]
   radio button to delete style and
   formatting codes in document.

   OR

   Select **Leave codes** radio button .... [L]
   to delete style but leave formatting in document.

6. Click [OK] .... [⏎]

7. Click [Close] .... [Esc]

Save Styles for Use in Other Documents

> NOTE: The complete list of styles is saved as a separate style file.

1. Click **Fo_r_mat**, **_S_tyles** .... `Alt`+`F8`

2. Click `O_ptions ▼` .... `Alt`+`O`, `F4`

3. Click **Save _A_s** .... `A`

4. Type style **_F_ilename** .... _filename_

> NOTE: WordPerfect saves style files in the Corel/Suite8/Template/Custom WP Templates folder. Click `⊟` to save in a different folder.

5. Select desired **Style type** option.

> NOTE: **_U_ser styles** are styles that you created. **System styles** are default WordPerfect styles used in the document, such as heading styles and footnote styles.

6. Click `OK` .... `↵`

7. Click `_C_lose` .... `Esc`

Retrieve Styles into Current Document

Copy styles from a template or from a styles file that you have created (see **Save Styles for Use in Other Documents**, page 109).

1. Click **Fo_r_mat**, **_S_tyles** .... `Alt`+`F8`

2. Click `O_ptions ▼` .... `Alt`+`O`, `F4`

3. Click **R_e_trieve** .... `E`

continued...

RETRIEVE STYLES INTO CURRENT DOCUMENT (CONTINUED)

4. Type style **Filename**...................................*filename*
   in text box, or select from drop–down list.

   NOTE: Click 🔲 *to open drop-down list.*

5. Click ⌗ OK ⌗ .... ⏎

6. Click ⌗ **Close** ⌗ .... Esc
   to return to document.

Create Graphics Style

1. Click **Format**, **Graphics Styles** .... Alt + R , G

2. Select desired **Style type** option.

3. Select desired **Styles** type .... ↑ ↓

4. Click ⌗ **Create...** ⌗ .... Alt + R

5. Type **Style name**................. Alt + N , *style name*
   in text box.

6. Select desired options for style type (e.g., caption
   style, border/fill style, position, content).

7. Click ⌗ OK ⌗ .... ⏎

8. Click ⌗ **Close** ⌗ .... Esc

Save Graphics Styles for Use in Other Documents

*Saves all styles of a particular type (such as fill styles) in the
current document into a separate styles file.*

1. Click **Format**, **Graphics Styles** .... Alt + R , G

2. Select desired **Style type** option.

continued...

3. Click `Options ▼` .... **Alt**+**O**, **F4**

4. Click **Save As** .... **A**

5. Type style **Filename** .... *style filename*

   NOTE: *WordPerfect saves style files in the Corel/Suite8/Template/Custom WP Templates folder. Click ▣ to save in a different folder.*

6. Click **OK** .... **↵**

7. Click **Close** .... **Esc**

Retrieve Graphics Styles

Copy styles from a styles file that you have created or from a template.

1. Click **Format**, **Graphics Styles** .... **Alt**+**R**, **G**

2. Click `Options ▼` .... **Alt**+**O**, **F4**

3. Click **Retrieve** .... **E**

4. Type **Filename** of template .... *filename*
   or styles file, or select from
   drop–down list.

   NOTE: *Click ▣ to open drop–down list.*

5. Click **OK** .... **↵**

6. Click **Close** .... **Esc**

SYMBOLS

Provides characters other than those found on the keyboard.

1. Place cursor where symbol(s) will be inserted.

2. Press **Ctrl+W**..⌜Ctrl⌟+⌜W⌟

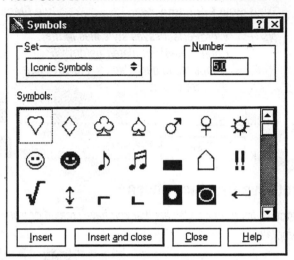

SYMBOLS DIALOG BOX

3. Select character **Set** .... ⌜Alt⌟+⌜S⌟, ⌜F4⌟, *letter*

4. Select from **Symbols**... ⌜Alt⌟+⌜M⌟, ⌜↑⌟⌜↓⌟⌜←⌟⌜→⌟

   *NOTE: To view more symbols in a character set, use the scroll bars or press **PgDn** and/or **PgUp**.*

5. Click ⌜ Insert ⌟ to insert symbol .... ⌜↵⌟
   and leave dialog box open. Repeat steps 3
   and 4 to insert another symbol as desired.

   OR

   Click ⌜ Insert and close ⌟ .... ⌜Alt⌟+⌜A⌟
   to insert symbol and close dialog box.

TABLE OF CONTENTS

To create a table of contents, you must complete the following three steps:

- **Mark text** *to include in table of contents.*

- **Define** *table of contents style and location.*

- **Generate** *the table of contents.*

All these procedures are described below.

Show Table of Contents Feature Bar

1. Click **Tools**, **Reference** .... `Alt`+`T`,`C`

2. Click **Table of Contents**................................. `T`

The Table of Contents feature bar appears.

Table of Contents level:	Mark 1	Mark 2	Mark 3	Mark 4	Mark 5	Define...	Generate...	Close

Mark Table of Contents Text

1. Select word(s) to include in table of contents.

2. Click **Mark #**................................ `Shift`+`Alt`+`#`
    (where # is the level number
    you are marking) to indicate
    level of entry.

3. Repeat steps 1 and 2 for every entry to add to
    table of contents.

Define Table of Contents

—WITH TABLE OF CONTENTS FEATURE BAR ACTIVE—

1. Place cursor where table of contents is to appear.

   NOTE: *To have the table appear on a new page,*
   *press **Ctrl+Enter** to insert a page break.*

2. Type title, if desired .... *title*
   (e.g., ᵀABLE OF CONTENTS).

3. Press **Enter** .... `⏎`

4. Click `Define...` .... `Shift`+`Alt`+`D`

5. Type desired **Number of Levels** .... *number*
   to include in table.

   To change page number position:

   Select format............ `Alt`+`#`, `F4`, `↑`, `↓`, `⏎`
   (where # is the **Level** number)
   for level(s) as desired.

   To format page numbers:

   a. Click `Page Numbering...` .... `Alt`+`P`

   b. Select **Document** page number format ...... `D`
      radio button.

      OR

      Click **Custom Page Format**........................ `U`
      and set up number format.

   NOTE: *Use the **Insert** button to add chapter*
   numbers or other types of numbering
   to a custom page format.

   c. Click `OK` .... `⏎`

continued ..

WordPerfect 115

To format level styles (font, indent, and other formatting for each level of entry):

a. Click [Styles...] .... **Alt**+**S**

b. Click **Level** to format............................ **↑** **↓**

c. Click [Edit] .... **Alt**+**E**

d. Add codes and text in **Contents** box using Styles Editor formatting options.

e. Click [OK] .... **↵**

f. Repeat from steps b-e to format other levels as desired.

g. Click [OK] .... **↵**

If creating table of contents with more than one level and the last level wrapped flush left (instead of indented):

Select **Display last level** .... **Alt**+**D**
in wrapped format check box.

NOTE: *If you select the option above, only the first three numbering formats are available for the last level. Also, all last level headings appear one after the other on the same line. Sample of the selected format is displayed in dialog box.*

6. Click [OK] .... **↵**

<<Table of Contents will generate here>> appears beneath your title.

NOTE: *If <<Table of Contents will generate here>> appears next to or above your title, you may move the title into the desired position.*

Generate Table of Contents

—WITH TABLE OF CONTENTS FEATURE BAR ACTIVE—

1. Click `Generate...` .... `Shift` + `Alt` + `G`

   NOTE: *If <<Table of Contents will generate here>> appears next to or above your title, you may move the title into the desired position.*

   If you have hypertext links in the document and wish to generate and save them:

   Select **Build hypertext links** check box .... `B`

2. Click `OK` .... `↵`

TABLES

Create Table Using QuickCreate

1. Position cursor where table will appear.

2. Click **Table QuickCreate** 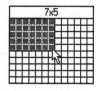 on toolbar and hold down mouse button to open drop-down table grid.

3. Drag across table grid to select desired number of rows/columns.

   NOTE: *Number at top of table grid shows number of columns and/or rows the table will have. For example, in the illustration of the drop-down grid (right), the table will have seven columns and five rows.*

4. Release mouse button.

Create Table Using Dialog Box

1. Position cursor where table will appear.

2. Press **F12** F12

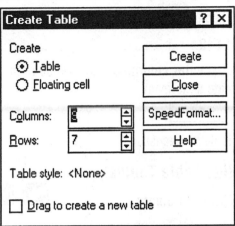

CREATE TABLE DIALOG BOX

3. Type or select number of **Columns** .... *number*

4. Type number of **Rows** .... Tab, *number*

   To apply table SpeedFormat if desired:

   a. Click SpeedFormat... .... Alt + E

   b. Click SpeedFormat to apply................... ↑ ↓
      from list box of **Available Style**.

   c. Click Apply .... ↵

5. Click Create... .... ↵

Convert Tabular or Parallel Columns to Table

Convert text separated by tabs or formatted using parallel columns to a table. (Newspaper columns are not considered parallel columns, so this procedure will not work for them.)

1. Select columns to convert.
2. Press **F12** .... `F12`
3. Select **T**abular column or **P**arallel column to create table from.
4. Click `OK` .... `↵`
5. Edit table as necessary.

Show/Hide Table Toolbar

1. Click **V**iew, **T**oolbars .... `Alt`+`V`, `T`
2. Click to select **Tables** check box from **A**vailable toolbars list.
3. Click `OK` .... `↵`

Table Cursor Movement

TO MOVE:	PRESS:
Next cell right	`Tab`
Previous cell left	`Shift`+`Tab`
Up or down one cell	`↑` `↓`
First cell in row	`Home`, `Home`
Last cell in row	`End`, `End`
Top line of cell	`Alt`+`Home`
Bottom line of cell	`Alt`+`End`

Insert Tab in Table Cells

NOTE: *Because the **Tab** key moves the cursor to the next cell, a hard tab must be used to insert a tab in a cell.*

TAB TYPE:	PRESS:
Hard Left Tab	Ctrl + Tab
Hard Decimal Tab	Alt + Shift + F7
Hard Back Tab	Ctrl + Shift + Tab

Select Table Cells Using Mouse

NOTE: *When cells are selected, the text in the cells is also selected, and you can use table structure or table format settings.*

USE QUICKSELECT IN A TABLE

In the table, move the cursor until it changes to a selection arrow: ⇦ or ⇧ :

To select a cell:

Click once.

To select a column or row:

Double-click.

To select the entire table:

Triple-click.

DESELECT ALL CELLS IN TABLE

Click any cell.

Insert Rows/Columns in Table

> NOTE: To insert one row above the current row,
> press **Alt+Ins**.

1. Right-click in table where rows/columns are to appear.

2. Click **I**nsert .... `I`

3. Type number of **R**ows .... `Tab`, *number*
   to insert in text box.

   OR

   a. Click **C**olumns .... `Alt`+`C`

   b. Type number of columns...................... *number*
      to insert in text box.

4. Click **B**efore... `Alt`+`B`
   to insert row/column before current
   cell (above row or to left of column).

   OR

   Click **A**fter .... `Alt`+`A`
   to insert row/column after current
   cell (below row or to right of column).

5. Click `OK` .... `⏎`

Delete Rows/Columns (Structure or Text)

1. Place cursor in column or row to delete,
   or select all desired cells.

   > NOTE: To delete entire table, select table. To
   > delete current row quickly, press **Alt+Del**.

2. Right–click mouse button.

3. Click **D**elete... `D`

   > NOTE: If you selected cells to delete, you don't
   > need to complete step 4; go directly to
   > step 5.

continued...

DELETE ROWS/COLUMNS (STRUCTURE/TEXT) (CONTINUED)

4. Type number of **Rows**...................... `Tab`, *number*
   to delete (current row and rows below).

   OR

   a. Click **Columns**.. `C`
   b. Type number of columns .... *number*
      to delete (current column
      and columns to right).

   To delete text only:

   Select **Cell contents only** radio button............. `E`

   To delete formulas only (keeps formula results):

   Select **Formulas only** radio button.................... `F`

5. Click ⬚ OK .... `↵`

Align Cell Contents

1. Place cursor in cell to format,
   or select cells to format.

2. Press **Ctrl+F12**...................................... `Ctrl`+`F12`

3. Click ⬚ Cell .... `Ctrl`+`Tab`
   if necessary.

4. Select **Horizontal** .... `F4`, `↑` `↓`, `↵`
   alignment desired.

5. Select **Vertical** .... `Alt`+`V`, `F4`, `↑` `↓`, `↵`
   alignment desired.

6. Click ⬚ OK .... `↵`

   *NOTE: You must view the document in Page
   view to see the new alignment.*

Adjust Horizontal Table Position

1. Press **Ctrl+F12** .... `Ctrl`+`F12`

2. Click `Table` .... `Ctrl`+`Tab`

3. Select desired .... `Alt`+`P`, `F4`, `↑`, `↓`, `↵`
   position from **Table position on page** list.

   If you selected From Left Edge in Step 3:

   Type or select distance .... `Tab`, *number*
   from left edge of paper
   to place the table.

   NOTE: *The **Left**, **Right**, **Center**, and **Full** settings*
                  place the table according to the margins
                  *(for example, **Full** extends the table from*
                  *the left to right margins while **Right** right-*
                  aligns the table).

4. Click `OK` .... `↵`

Change Table Size and Column Width Using Ruler

1. Place cursor in table.

   To display ruler (if necessary):

   Press **Alt+Shift+F3** .... `Alt`+`Shift`+`F3`

2. Drag table (margin marker) and ▼ (column width markers) on ruler.

Format Table Borders/Fills

*Tables have two kinds of lines: **Table Borders** outside a selected rectangle of cells, and **Cell Borders** inside a selected rectangle of cells.*

1. Select cells if applying borders or shading to particular cells.

2. Press **Shift+F12** .... `Shift`+`F12`

3. Click `Table` .... `Ctrl`+`Tab`
   to apply borders/shading to entire table.
   OR
   Click `Cell` .... `Ctrl`+`Tab`
   to apply borders/shading for selected cells.

4. Set options as desired.

5. Click `Apply` .... `Alt`+`A`

   NOTE: *After formatting, you can move the dialog box (drag the title bar) to view the formatting in your table. Then, you can continue formatting.*

6. Click `OK` .... `↵`

Show/Hide Row and Column Indicators

Shows or hides row number and column letter headings.

1. Right-click table.

2. Click **Row/Column Indicators** .... `U`

Split Cell

1. Right-click cell to split.

2. Click **Split Cell** .... `S`

continued...

SPLIT CELL (CONTINUED)

3. Type or select number...................`Tab`, *number* of **Columns** to **Divide into**.

OR

Type or select number.............`Alt`+`R`, *number* of **Rows** to **Divide into**.

4. Click [OK]...`↵`

> *NOTE:*   *To remove split, follow **Join Cells** procedure, on the following page.*

Join Cells

1. Select cells to join into single cell.

2. Right-click table.

3. Click **Join Cells**...`J`

Lock/Unlock Cells

Lock cells to prevent cell contents from being altered.

1. Place cursor in cell to (un)lock, or select desired cells.

2. Press **Ctrl+F12**.....................................`Ctrl`+`F12`

3. Click [Cell].......................................`Ctrl`+`Tab` if necessary.

4. Select/deselect **Lock cell to**........... ....`Alt`+`L` **prevent change** check box.

5. Click [OK]..`↵`

Repeating Table Headers

Sets a specified number of rows in a table (beginning with row 1) to repeat at the top of each subsequent page if a table continues on multiple pages.

1. Select row(s) that contain headers.

2. Press **Ctrl+F12**.................................. `Ctrl`+`F12`

3. Select **Header row** check box .... `R`

4. Click `OK` .... `↵`

TABS

Set/Clear Tabs

1. Place cursor where tab settings should begin.

   OR

   Select paragraphs to set tabs.

2. Click **Format**, **Line** .... `Alt`+`R`, `L`

3. Click **Tab Set**... `T`

4. Select desired **Tab type**.............. `F4`, `↑`, `↓`, `↵`

The tab type determines the alignment of text at the tab. For example, a Right tab type right-aligns text at the tab.

5. Type or select **Tab position**...... `Alt`+`P`, *number*

continued...

SET/CLEAR TABS (CONTINUED)

6. Select desired "position from" radio button option:

- **from left margin (relative)**.............. Alt + M
  to set tab stops relative to left margin.

- **from left edge of paper (absolute)**.. Alt + E
  to set tab stops measured from left edge of page.

7. Select other options as desired.

8. Click [OK] .... ↵

Change Decimal Align Character

1. Place cursor where tab settings should begin.
   OR
   Select paragraphs to set tabs.

2. Click **Format, Line**.......................... Alt + R , L

3. Click **Tab Set**... T

4. Click **Character to align on** text box....... Alt + R

5. Type new alignment character................. *character* if necessary.

6. Click [OK] .... ↵

Insert Hard Tab

1. Place cursor where hard tab is to appear.

2. Click **Format, Line**.......................... Alt + R , L

3. Click **Other Codes** .... O

4. Select desired hard tab to insert from **Hard tabs** or **Hard tabs with dot leaders** radio button options.

5. Click [Insert] .... ↵

TEMPLATES

*A **template** is a reusable document that lets you create an unlimited number of new documents in the customized format. It may contain text, graphics, styles, macros, abbreviations, and other elements. All of these elements appear in documents that you create using the template.*

All documents are based on templates. When you create a document without specifying a template, the new document is based on the default template, WP8US.WPT.

Some templates are called PerfectExpert projects. These are templates for predefined document types, such as newsletters and memos.

Edit Template

1. Click **File**, **New**.................................. `Ctrl`+`Shift`+`N`

2. Click drop-down arrow ▼ .... `F4`
   at top of dialog box to open
   list of template types.

3. Click desired template category.

   Displays templates in the category you selected.

4. Click template to edit.

   NOTE: Not all templates listed are actually installed on your computer.

5. Click [Options ▼] .... `Alt`+`P`

6. Click **Edit WP Template**............................... `I`

   NOTE: If you get an error message, the template is not installed. Rerun setup to install the template.

continued...

EDIT TEMPLATE (CONTINUED)

7. Change template as desired.

   NOTE: *For example, set the default formatting, add headers and footers, add a graphic, such as a company logo, or add any other text, graphics, or formatting that you would like to be included in documents that you create based on this template.*

8. Click **File**, **Save** .... `Ctrl` + `S`

9. Click **File**, **Close** when finished .... `Ctrl` + `F4`

TEXTART

Creates special text images, including waves, pennants, circles, crescents, or bow ties. Images can be further enhanced with shadows, outline text, fills, and rotation.

Create TextArt

1. Click **Insert**, **Graphics** .... `Alt` + `I`, `G`

2. Click **TextArt** .... `X`

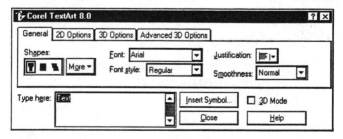

COREL TEXTART 8.0 DIALOG BOX

3. Type text in **Type here** text box .... *text*

4. Click desired shape in **Shapes** list.

   OR

   Click `More ▼` and click desired shape.

continued...

5. Select font and justification options.

6. Click **3D Mode**, if desired .... <kbd>Alt</kbd>+<kbd>3</kbd>

   *NOTE: You can apply 3D special effects only if you installed TextArt 3D mode during installation. If you apply 3D, use the **3D Options** and **Advanced 3D Options** tabs to customize 3D effects for the current drawing.*

   OR

   Click <kbd>2D Options</kbd> and set patterns, shadows, rotation, and other options as desired.

7. Click <kbd>Close</kbd> .... <kbd>Alt</kbd>+<kbd>C</kbd>
   to exit and insert the picture in the document.

Edit TextArt

1. Double–click TextArt to edit.

2. Edit image as desired, following steps 3–7 of **Create TextArt**, page 40.

THESAURUS

Look Up Synonym or Antonym

1. Place cursor anywhere on word.

2. Press **Alt+F1** .... <kbd>Alt</kbd>+<kbd>F1</kbd>

   To replace word in document with synonym/antonym:

   a. Select desired synonym or antonym.

   b. Click <kbd>Replace</kbd> .... <kbd>Alt</kbd>+<kbd>R</kbd>

   c. Select desired word...................... <kbd>↑</kbd> <kbd>↓</kbd> , <kbd>↵</kbd>
      from **Word Forms** list box.

continued...

To show additional, related words:

Double–click word in list.

WordPerfect displays words in a new column.

To type word to look up:

a. Click **Re̲place With** text box .... `Alt`+`E`

b. Type word .... *text*

c. Click ⎡ Look U̲p ⎤ .... `Alt`+`U`

3. Click ⎡ C̲lose ⎤ .... `Alt`+`C`
   if necessary.

TOOLBARS

Lets you use the mouse to access frequently used commands.

Display/Hide Toolbar

1. Click **V̲iew**, **T̲oolbars** .... `Alt`+`V`, `T`

2. Click check box next to toolbar to display or hide.

A check mark ✓ next to items on submenus means the feature is active/visible.

TYPEOVER/INSERT MODE

Switches keyboard entry mode from Typeover to Insert. Use Typeover mode to replace existing characters to the right of the cursor as you type. Switch back to Insert mode (the default mode) for text to move ahead of the cursor as you type.

Press **Insert** .... `Insert`
to switch between Typeover and Insert mode.

WordPerfect

UNDELETE

Allows you to view and/or restore your last three deletions.

Restore Deletions

1. Place cursor where deletion took place.

2. Press **Ctrl+Shift+Z** .... Ctrl + Shift + Z

Last deletion appears as selected text at cursor.

3. Select desired option button(s) on
    Undelete dialog box:

UNDO

Reverses the last change made to a document, such as text you have typed or deleted, or formats you have changed. Does not reverse maneuvering actions, such as mouse and cursor or scrolling movements.

> *NOTE: To see which action will be undone or reversed, place pointer over toolbar button. Pop-up tip displays.*

Undo Last Action

Click **Undo**  .... Ctrl + Z

Redo Action (Reverses Last Undo)

Click **Redo**  .... Ctrl + Shift + R

VIEWS

*There are three views available from the **View** menu.*

- **Draft**   Basic text imitates WYSIWYG, but features such as headers, footers, and watermarks do not appear. Therefore, this option is usually faster than Page view. Press **Ctrl+F5**.

- **Page**   Displays a full WYSIWYG. Features such as headers, footers, and watermarks appear. Items that do not print, such as comments, appear as icons. Press **Alt+F5**.

  *NOTE: Use **Zoom** (**Alt+V, Z**) to change the display size of text or graphics for the above views.*

- **Two Pages**   Shows two pages at a time. The format is similar to Page view, above. Press **Alt+V**, **W**.

  *NOTE: Use **Tools**, **Settings**, **Display**, **View/Zoom** tab to set the default view.*

WATERMARK

Adds a faint image or drawing behind printed text.

You can have two watermarks in a document, called Watermarks A and B.

> *NOTES: If you create Watermark A and Watermark B on the same page, they are superimposed.*
>
> *You can create (but not view) watermarks in Draft view. To see the watermark on the page, use Page view or Two Pages view.*

Create Watermark

NOTE: *You can type text (such as "Confidential" or "Draft") to use as a watermark, or you can insert an existing graphic–such as clip art. WordPerfect clip art is located in the Corel\Suite8\Graphics\ClipArt folder.*

1. Click **Insert**, **Watermark**................ `Alt`+`I`, `W`

2. Select **Watermark A** or **B** .... `A` or `B`

3. Click `Create` .... `↵`

   To insert clipart:

   a. Click **Clipart** 🔲 .... `Alt`+`I`, `G`, `C`

   b. Drag picture from **Scrapbook** to page.

   c. Click ☒ in title bar of **Scrapbook** window to close Scrapbook.

   To insert a graphic file:

   a. Click **Insert**, **Graphics** .... `Alt`+`I`, `G`

   b. Click **From File** .... `F`

   c. Double-click file to insert.

   To insert TextArt:

   Follow **Create TextArt** procedure, page 40.

   To insert text box:

   a. Click **Insert**, **Text Box**................ `Alt`+`I`, `X`

   b. Type and format text, as desired.

   c. Click `Close` .... `Alt`+`Shift`+`C`

continued...

CREATE WATERMARK (CONTINUED)

4. Right-click watermark and use QuickMenu to adjust watermark **Size**, **Position**, and other settings.

    NOTE: Commands on QuickMenu vary depending on the type of object.

5. Press **Ctrl+F4** .... `Ctrl`+`F4`
    to return to document.

Discontinue Watermark

1. Place cursor in first page where watermark should not appear.

    NOTE: Watermark will appear on previous page(s).

2. Click **Insert**, **Watermark** .... `Alt`+`I`, `W`

3. Select **Watermark A** or **B** to discontinue.

4. Click `Discontinue` .... `D`

Delete Watermark

1. Turn on Reveal Codes screen
    *(see **Reveal Codes**, page 96).*

2. Position Reveal Codes window cursor on
    `Watermark A` or `Watermark B`

    *NOTE: To search for a Watermark code, see **Find Word(s) or Code(s)**, page 27.*

3. Press **Delete** .... `Delete`

WIDOW/ORPHAN

*(See **Keep Text Together**, page 59.)*

WordPerfect 135

WORDPERFECT SETTINGS

1. Click **Tools**, **Settings**...................... Alt + T, N

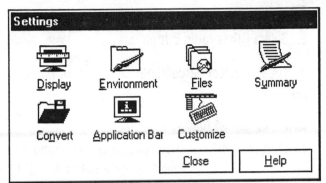

SETTINGS DIALOG BOX

2. Double–click desired icon .... Alt +*letter,* ↵

3. Make desired changes.

4. Click [OK] .... ↵

5. Click [Close] .... Esc

ZOOM

Controls the size of text and graphics as they appear on your screen.

> *NOTES:* *This feature does not change the size of printed text and graphics.*
>
> *Use* **Tools**, **Settings**, **Display**, **View/Zoom** *tab to set the default zoom.*

1. Click **View**, **Zoom**............................ Alt + V, Z

continued...

ZOOM (CONTINUED)

2. Select percentage to zoom ....*number*

    OR

    a. Select **Other** radio button .... ⌐Alt⌐+⌐O⌐

    b. Type or select percentage............ ⌐Tab⌐, *number*

    OR

    Select option as follows:

    - **Margin width**   Displays text within window,
      minimal white space on right
      and left.

    - **Page width**   Displays width of page within
      window, including margins.

    - **Full page**   Displays all page margins
      within window (left, right, top,
      and bottom).

3. Click ⌐ OK ⌐ .... ⌐↵⌐

CELL BLOCKS

Insert Block

INSERT COLUMN

1. Select as many column(s) as you will insert.

   *NOTE: Selected column(s) will move to the right
   to insert the new columns.*

2. Click **Insert** ⊞ .... `Alt` + `I`, `L`

   *NOTE: If you do not select column(s) in step 1,
   the **Insert Cells** dialog box opens as
   shown In **Insert Cell(s)** procedure, below.*

INSERT ROW(S)

1. Select as many rows as you will insert.

   *NOTE: Selected row(s) will move down to insert
   new rows.*

2. Click **Insert** ⊞ .... `Alt` + `I`, `R`

   *NOTE: If you do not select row(s) in step 1, the
   Insert Cells dialog box opens as shown in
   Insert Cell(s) procedure, below.*

INSERT CELL(S)

1. Select as many cells as you will insert.

   *NOTE: Selected cell(s) will move to make room
   for new cells.*

2. Click **Insert** ⊞ .... `Alt` + `I`, `C`

continued...

INSERT CELLS (CONTINUED)

```
┌─────────────────────────────────────────────┐
│ Insert Cells                          [?][X] │
│                                              │
│  Cells:                        ┌──────────┐  │
│  ┌────────────────────────┐    │    OK    │  │
│  │ A:D10..F19          [R]│    └──────────┘  │
│  └────────────────────────┘    ┌──────────┐  │
│  ┌Dimension──┐ ┌Span──────┐    │  Cancel  │  │
│  │ ○ Columns │ │ ◉ Entire │    └──────────┘  │
│  │ ◉ Rows    │ │ ○ Partial│    ┌──────────┐  │
│  │ ○ Sheets  │ │          │    │   Help   │  │
│  └───────────┘ └──────────┘    └──────────┘  │
└─────────────────────────────────────────────┘
```

INSERT CELLS DIALOG BOX

3. Select **Columns** radio button.............. `Alt`+`L`
   to move selected cells to right
   of new cells.

   OR

   Select **Rows** radio button.................. `Alt`+`R`
   to move selected cells down
   from new cells.

4. Click **Partial** radio button................ `Alt`+`A`

5. Click `OK` .... `↵`

INSERT SHEET

1. Click sheet tab.

   *NOTE: The new sheet will be inserted at the
   current sheet location. The current
   sheet will move back one.*

2. Click **Insert, Sheet** .... `Alt`+`I`,`T`

Delete Block

*These procedures delete entire cells, moving existing cells to fill in the deleted space. To delete the contents of cells, rather than the cells themselves—use the **Delete** key or the **Edit**, **Clear** command.*

Deleting a cell containing a coordinate cell that defines a named block causes the name to become invalid. Any formulas or names that reference the block display ERR, indicating an error. Deleting a cell referenced in a formula causes the formula to register as ERR.

DELETE COLUMN(S)

1. Select column(s) to delete.

   NOTE: The column(s) to the right will move to fill in the space left by the deleted columns.

2. Click **Delete** 🗐 .... `Alt`+`E`, `D`

   *NOTE: If you do not select column(s) in step 1, the **Delete** dialog box opens as shown in **Delete Cell(s)** procedure, on next page.*

DELETE ROW(S)

1. Select row(s) to delete.

   NOTE: The remaining rows will move up to close up space.

2. Click **Delete** 🗐 .... `Alt`+`E`, `D`

   *NOTE: If you do not select row(s) in step 1, the **Delete** dialog box opens as shown in **Delete Cell(s)** procedure, on next page.*

DELETE CELL(S)

1. Select cell(s) to delete.

   *NOTE: The remaining cells will move left if you
   delete a column block, or up if you delete
   a row block.*

2. Click **Delete** ⊞ .... Alt + E , D

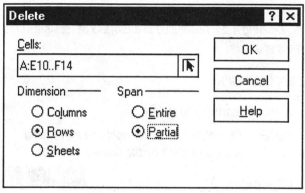

DELETE DIALOG BOX

3. Select **Columns** radio button................. Alt + L
   to move cells to left to close up space.

   OR

   Select **Rows** radio button...................... Alt + R
   to move cells up to close up space.

4. Select **Partial** radio button..................... Alt + A

5. Click ⟨ OK ⟩ .... ↵

DELETE SHEET

1. Right-click sheet tab of sheet to delete.

2. Click **Delete Sheet**............................... D

Name Block

CREATE BLOCK NAME

1. Highlight cell(s) to name.
2. Click **I**nsert, **N**ame, **C**ells .... `Ctrl`+`F3`
3. Type block **N**ame...*name*

   NOTE: *Name can be up to 15 characters. Do not*
   use operators (+,-, =, #, *, /, ^, <, >, &, $),
   parentheses, or spaces. Do not use names
   that are already in use.

4. Click `Add` .... `↵`
5. Click `Close` .... `Esc`

CREATE BLOCK NAMES FROM ADJACENT LABELS

For example, you could name a column with a label (title) that
appears at the top of the column.

1. Highlight cell(s) to name.
2. Click **I**nsert, **N**ame, **C**ells .... `Ctrl`+`F3`
3. Click `Labels...` .... `Alt`+`L`
4. Specify block to use as names in **C**ells text box.
5. Select desired **Directions** radio button option to
   show location of cells in relation to labels in the
   selected block.

   NOTE: *For example, if you are naming a column*
   using the label at the top of the column, you
   *would select the **D**own radio button option.*

6. Click `OK` .... `↵`
7. Click `Close` .... `Esc`

CREATE TABLE OF NAMED BLOCKS

1. Highlight upper–left cell of block where you wish to place table in an empty area of a sheet.

2. Click **I**nsert, **N**ame, **C**ells .... `Ctrl`+`F3`

3. Click `Output...` .... `Alt`+`O`

4. Click `OK` .... `↵`

   NOTES: *The table requires two columns and one row for each block name.*

   Named blocks *appear in alphabetical order in the table.*

5. Click `Close` .... `Esc`

DELETE BLOCK NAME

1. Click **I**nsert, **N**ame, **C**ells .... `Ctrl`+`F3`

2. Click block name...................... `Tab`, `Tab`, `↑` `↓`
   to delete in **N**ame list box.

   OR

   Type block name to delete...........................*name*
   in **N**ame text box.

3. Click `Delete` .... `Alt`+`D`

4. Click `Close` .... `Esc`

DELETE ALL BLOCK NAMES

1. Click **I**nsert, **N**ame, **C**ells .... `Ctrl`+`F3`

2. Click `Delete All` .... `Alt`+`E`

continued...

DELETE ALL BLOCK NAMES (CONTINUED)

3. Click [Yes] .... [Y]

    to delete all names.

    OR

    Click [No] .... [↵]

4. Click [Close] .... [Esc]

Sort Block

USE MENU TO SORT

1. Highlight data block to sort.

    *NOTES: To specify a sort order using labels
    (headings) instead of cell addresses,
    include labels in the selection.*

    *This procedure does not sort labels—they
    will remain where they are.*

2. Click **Tools, Sort** .... [Alt]+[T], [T]

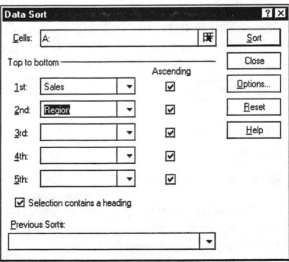

DATA SORT DIALOG BOX

continued...

USE MENU TO SORT (CONTINUED)

To sort by field names/labels:

Select **Selection contains a heading** check box, if necessary.

3. Type/select first column/row.... `Alt`+`1` , `↑` `↓` to sort on in **1st** Sort Key box.

4. Specify sort order:

To sort in ascending order:

Leave default check mark in **Ascending** check box.

To sort in descending order:

Click **Ascending** box to clear default check mark.

5. Repeat steps 3 and 4 for remaining sort keys, as desired.

To sort rows rather than columns:

a. Click `Options...` .... `Alt`+`O`

b. Select **Left to right** radio button .... `L`

c. Click `OK` .... `↵`

6. Click `Sort` .... `Alt`+`S`

USE TOOLBAR TO SORT

Sorts by column.

1. Highlight data block to sort.

2. Press **Shift+Ctrl** and click .... `Shift`+`Ctrl`+*click* each column to sort by (starting with first sort order).

continued...

Quattro Pro 145

3. Right-click toolbar.

4. Click **Selection Formatting** .... $\boxed{S}$, $\boxed{↵}$
   to change toolbar.

   To sort in ascending order:

   Click top half (A...Z) **Sort** $\boxed{\begin{smallmatrix}A...Z\\Z...A\end{smallmatrix}}$ of Block Manipulation toolbar.

   To sort in descending order:

   Click bottom half (Z...A) **Sort** $\boxed{\begin{smallmatrix}A...Z\\Z...A\end{smallmatrix}}$ of Block Manipulation toolbar.

5. Right-click toolbar.

6. Click **Selection Formatting** .... $\boxed{S}$, $\boxed{↵}$
   to return to default toolbar.

Transpose Columns and Rows

Converts rows to columns or vice versa.

1. Select desired block to copy and transpose.

2. Click **Tools**, **Numeric Tools** .... $\boxed{Alt}$+$\boxed{T}$, $\boxed{N}$

3. Click **Transpose** .... $\boxed{T}$

4. Type address of upper–left cell .... *address*
   of destination block in **To** text box, if necessary.

5. Click $\boxed{\text{OK}}$ .... $\boxed{↵}$

   CAUTION: *Be sure the block being transposed does not contain formulas with relative cell references. All references should be absolute.*

COPY AND MOVE

Copy to Clipboard

1. Highlight data to copy.

2. Press **Ctrl+C** .... `Ctrl`+`C`

    NOTE: *Once the data is on the Windows Clipboard, it can be pasted elsewhere. (See* **Paste from Clipboard**, *below.)*

Cut to Clipboard

1. Highlight data to move.

2. Press **Ctrl+X** .... `Ctrl`+`X`

    NOTE: *Once the data is on the Windows Clipboard, it can be pasted elsewhere. (See* **Paste from Clipboard**, *below.)*

Paste from Clipboard

    NOTE: *The Clipboard must contain copied or cut data.*

1. Place cursor in upper–left corner of location where you want block to be pasted.

2. Press **Ctrl+V** .... `Ctrl`+`V`

Paste Special

Determines which cell attributes to paste—such as whether or not to include cell comments and properties. You can also use this procedure to paste the values of formulas rather than the actual formulas themselves.

    NOTE: *The Clipboard must contain copied or cut data.*

1. Place cursor in upper–left corner of location where you want to paste data.

2. Click **E**dit, **Paste S**pecial .... `Alt`+`E`, `S`

continued...

Quattro Pro

```
┌─────────────────────────────────────────────┐
│ Paste Special                      [?][X]    │
│ ┌─Paste─────────────────┐  ┌──────────────┐  │
│ │ ☑ Formula Cells       │  │    Paste     │  │
│ │ ☑ Label Cells         │  ├──────────────┤  │
│ │ ☑ Number Cells        │  │    Link      │  │
│ │ ☑ Properties          │  ├──────────────┤  │
│ │ ☐ Cell Comments       │  │   Cancel     │  │
│ └───────────────────────┘  ├──────────────┤  │
│ ┌─Options───────────────┐  │    Help      │  │
│ │ ☐ Avoid Pasting Blanks│  └──────────────┘  │
│ │ ☐ Transpose Rows and Columns             │  │
│ │ ☐ Paste Formulas as Values               │  │
│ └───────────────────────────────────────┘   │
└─────────────────────────────────────────────┘
```

PASTE SPECIAL DIALOG BOX

3. Clear the check mark (✓) from any attributes that you do *not* want to **Paste**.

   NOTE: All checked items will be included.

4. Select from **Options** as follows:

   - **Avoid Pasting Blanks** — Will not overwrite existing data in a destination if the data will be replaced by a blank cell in the cells to paste.

   - **Transpose Rows and Columns** — Converts rows to columns.

   - **Paste Formulas as Values** — Pastes the results of formulas (their calculated values) but not the formulas themselves.

5. Click [Paste] .... [↵]

   OR

   Click [Link] .... [Alt]+[L]

   NOTE: If you click the Link button, any changes that you make to the original cells are reflected in the pasted cells.

Copy Formulas and Adjust Absolute References

1. Select cell(s) to copy.

2. Click **E**dit, **Cop**y Cells...................... `Alt`+`E`,`Y`

3. Type destination block in **T**o text box.

    To adjust absolute references to new locations:

    Click **M**odel Copy check box.................. `Alt`+`M`

4. Click ⌈   OK   ⌉... `↵`

Move Cells by Dragging

1. Select cell(s) to move.

2. Position pointer at edge of block (e.g., right or bottom border) until pointer changes to four-headed arrow.

3. Drag to new position.

Move Sheet

Drag desired sheet tab to new location.

Create File from Copied Cells

Creates a new notebook by copying selected cells in the current notebook. You can copy formulas or just formula results (converts formulas to their values in the new notebook).

1. Select cells to extract.

    NOTE: The selected data will appear in the new notebook starting at cell A1, regardless of its position in the current notebook.

2. Click **T**ools, **D**ataTools.................... `Alt`+`T`,`D`

continued...

CREATE FILE FROM COPIED CELLS (CONTINUED)

3. Click **Extract to File**...............................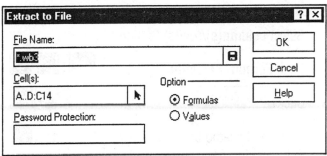

EXTRACT TO FILE DIALOG BOX

4. Type **File Name** to create...............................*name*
   from extracted cells.

   *NOTE: To create a text file (rather than a
   notebook, *.wb3 file), use the .txt
   file extension.*

5. Select **Formulas** radio buttons............... Alt+O
   to include all cell data, including
   formulas, If necessary.

   OR

   Select **Values** radio buttons................... Alt+A
   to convert formulas to
   their values in new file.

6. Type password............... Alt+P, *password,* ⏎
   to assign **Password Protection**
   to destination file, if desired.

   *NOTE: If you selected **Password Protection**,
   you will need to verify the password.*

7. Click ⬚ OK .... ⏎

DISPLAY
Hide Data

HIDE ROWS/COLUMNS

1. Select column(s)/row(s) to hide.

2. Click **Fo_r_mat**, **S_e_lection** .... `Alt`+`R`, `E`

3. Click `Row/Column` .... `Ctrl`+`Tab`

4. Select **Hi_de** radio button .... `I`
   to hide column(s).

   OR

   Select **Hi_de** radio button .... `D`
   to hide row(s).

5. Click `OK` .... `↵`

SHOW HIDDEN ROWS/COLUMNS

1. Select row(s)/column(s) on both
   sides of hidden row(s)/column(s).

2. Click **Fo_r_mat**, **S_e_lection** .... `Alt`+`R`, `E`

3. Click `Row/Column` .... `Ctrl`+`Tab`

4. Select **Re_v_eal** radio button .... `V`
   to show column(s).

   OR

   Click **Reveal_** radio button .... `L`
   to show row(s).

5. Click `OK` .... `↵`

Filter Data

APPLY QUICKFILTER

Shows only the data that meets the criteria that you specify.

1. Display sheet to filter.
2. Click **Tools**, **QuickFilter** .... `Alt`+`T`, `U`
3. Click ▾ in column to filter.
4. Click data to view bottom of list .... `↓`
   (only selected data will appear).
5. Repeat steps 3 and 4 to specify criteria
   for other columns as desired.

   *NOTE: For example, you might want to see only
   the West Region for First Quarter sales.*

APPLY TOP–TEN QUICKFILTER

*Shows only the data for the top ten numbers in a numeric field.
For example, using this feature, you could view the top–ten
selling wines.*

1. Display sheet to filter.
2. Click **Tools**, **QuickFilter** .... `Alt`+`T`, `U`
3. Click ▾ in column to filter.
4. Click **[Top 10...]** .... `↓`, `↵`
5. Click `OK` .... `↵`
6. Follow **Apply QuickFilter** procedure, steps 3-5, if
   desired, to apply more criteria.

   *NOTE: For example, you might want to see the
   top–ten wine sales in the West Region only.*

REMOVE QUICKFILTER

Click **Tools**, **QuickFilter** .... `Alt`+`T`, `U`

Show/Hide Row and Column Borders

1. Right-click sheet tab to format.

2. Click **Sheet Properties**.................. . ... `S`

3. Click `Display` if necessary .... `Ctrl`+`Tab`

4. Select **Row Borders** check box, if desired .... `R`

5. Select **Column Borders** check box, if desired ...... `C`

6. Click `OK` .... `↵`

Show/Hide Grid Lines

1. Right-click sheet tab to format.

2. Click **Sheet Properties**............................. `S`

3. Click `Display` .... `Ctrl`+`Tab`

4. Select/deselect desired **Grid Lines** check box
   option(s), **Horizontal** and/or **Vertical**.

5. Click `OK` .... `↵`

Set Display of Zeros

*Cells with zero values appear as blank cells when the **No** radio button is selected (step 4, below).*

1. Right-click sheet tab to format.

2. Click **Sheet Properties**............................. `S`

3. Click `Display` .... `Ctrl`+`Tab`

4. Select desired **Display Zeros** option .... `Y` or `N`

5. Click `OK` .... `↵`

Show/Hide Application Items

Show or hide toolbars, Property Bar, Application Bar, and other settings.

1. Click **Tools**, **Settings** .... `Alt`+`T`, `E`

2. Click `Display` if necessary .... `Ctrl`+`Tab`

3. Set **Display Options** as desired.

4. Click `OK` .... `↵`

Lock/Unlock Titles

Locks rows and/or columns that contain titles. When you scroll, the locked area remains on the screen. Repeat this procedure to unlock. Locked rows and columns do not affect printing.

1. Select left-most cell in row below the one to lock.

   OR

   Select top cell in column to right of one to lock.

   OR

   Select upper-left cell beneath and to the right of columns/rows to lock (locks rows above and columns to the left of the selected cell).

2. Click **View**, **Locked Titles** .... `Alt`+`V`, `L`

3. Click `OK` .... `↵`

Display Objects Sheet

*The **Objects sheet** lists all charts, slide shows, and custom dialog boxes in the notebook. Use the Objects sheet to copy or print objects and to create charts, slide shows, and dialog boxes.*

GO TO OBJECTS SHEET

Click **V**iew, **O**bjects .... 【Alt】+【V】,【O】

> NOTE: *You can double–click any object icon to edit it.*

RETURN TO PREVIOUS SHEET

Click **V**iew, **D**raft .... 【Alt】+【V】,【D】

Zoom

1. Click **V**iew, **Z**oom............................ 【Alt】+【V】,【Z】

2. Select desired percentage option to zoom in/out.

   OR

   Type **C**ustom zoom percentage.......... 【C】, *number*

3. Click 【 OK 】 .... 【↵】

Split Window

SPLIT WINDOW INTO PANES

1. Click **V**iew, **S**plit **W**indow .... 【Alt】+【V】,【W】

2. Select desired **Pane Options** radio button, **Hori**zontal or **V**ertical.

3. Click 【 OK 】 .... 【↵】

The default setting synchronizes pane scrolling in the direction panes are divided. If the panes are divided vertically, they scroll vertically simultaneously. If they are divided horizontally, they scroll horizontally simultaneously.

Go to Next Pane

Press **F6** .... `F6`

Remove Panes

1. Click **V**iew, Split **W**indow .... `Alt` + `V` , `W`

2. Select **C**lear radio button .... `C`

3. Click | OK | .... `↵`

EDIT

Enter Data in Cell

The data that you type appears in the active cell and in the input line (just above the sheet).

1. Click cell.

2. Press **F2** to activate Edit mode .... `F2`

3. Type cell data .... *data*

    To use Point mode to enter cell addresses in formula:

    a. Press **F2** to activate Point mode .... `F2`

    b. Select cells on sheet.

    c. Press **F2** to enter address of selected .... `F2`
        cells in formula and return to Edit mode.

    To enter block name in formula:

    a. Position cursor after an operator .... `F2`

    b. Press **F3** .... `F3`

    c. Double-click name .... `↑` `↓` , `↵`
        to enter in formula.

continued...

ENTER DATA IN CELL (CONTINUED)

To insert function name:

a. Press **Alt+F3** .... `Alt` + `F3`

b. Click desired **Function** .... `Alt` + `C` , `↑` `↓`
   Category to list.

c. Double-click **Function** ...... `Alt` + `F` , `↑` `↓` , `↵`
   to insert in formula.

4. Press **Enter** to end Edit mode .... `↵`

Add Column/Row Cell Data

Creates a formula using @SUM function to total selected cells.

1. Select contiguous cells in column/row plus one
   blank cell at the end of the selection.

   NOTE: The blank cell will contain the sum.

2. Click **QuickSum** `Σ`

Change Enter Key Action

*By default, when you press **Enter**, the cell selector moves to
the next cell below. Use this procedure to have the cell selector
remain in the same cell when you press **Enter**.*

1. Click **Tools**, **Settings** .... `Alt` + `T` , `E`

2. Click `General` .... `Ctrl` + `Tab`

3. Deselect **Move Cell Selector on Enter Key** ...... `M`
   check box option.

4. Click `OK` .... `↵`

Go To

1. Click **Edit**, **Go To** F5

2. Type address of destination cell .... *address*
   in **Reference** text box.

   OR

   Select named range .... Alt + C , ↑ ↓
   to go to from **Cell Names** box.

3. Click [OK] .... ↵

Undo Last Action

Click **Edit**, **Undo Last Action** .... Ctrl + Z

> *NOTE:* The **Undo** command on **Edit** menu shows
> the action that will be reversed.

Delete Cell Data

*Deletes cell data (including values, formulas, and text), leaving
comments, formatting, and other cell attributes intact.*

1. Select cell(s) containing data to delete.

2. Press **Backspace** or **Delete** .... Backspace or Delete

Clear Cells

1. Select cell(s) with data/formatting to delete.

2. Click **Edit**, **Clear** .... Alt + E , E

3. Click desired Clear option:

   - **Cells**   to erase data, comments, and
                      formatting.

   - **Values**   to erase data only.

   - **Formats**   to remove formatting only.

   - **Comments**   to erase comments only.

Replace Formulas with Values

Replaces selected formulas with their calculated values (formulas are erased but values remain).

1. Select cell(s) containing formulas.

2. Click **Edit**, **Convert to Values** .... `Alt`+`E`, `V`

   NOTE: *Do not change **From** or **To** addresses/ranges.*

3. Click `OK` .... `↵`

Insert Current Date

Click **Insert**, **Date** .... `Alt`+`I`, `D`

    NOTE: *To apply a different date format (change the appearance of the date data), click **Format**, **Selection**, **Numeric Format** tab.*

Fill Cells with Incremental Data

1. In first cells of series, type starting sequential data (called *seed values*).

  EXAMPLES:

5		Sunday		1ˢᵗ
10		Monday		2ⁿᵈ

2. Highlight cells to fill, including cells containing seed values.

3. Click **Edit**, **Fill**, **QuickFill** .... `Alt`+`E`, `I`, `Q`

Quattro Pro fills selected cells with series.

Quattro Pro

Cell Comments

ADD COMMENT TO CELL

1. Click cell to comment on.

2. Click **Insert**, **Comment** .... `Alt` + `I` , `M`

3. Type comment .... *comment*

   To format comment font attributes:

   a. Right-click inside comment bubble.

   b. Click **Cell Comment Properties** .... `C`

   c. Set **Typeface**, **Point Size**, and emphasis **Options** as desired.

   d. Click ` OK ` .... `↵`

4. Click outside comment bubble .... `Esc`

   NOTE: Cells containing a comment display a red triangle in the upper-right corner of the cell.

DISPLAY COMMENT

NOTE: Cells containing a comment display a red triangle in the upper-right corner of the cell.

Place mouse pointer over cell containing comment.

EDIT COMMENT

1. Click cell containing comment.

2. Click **Insert**, **Comment** .... `Alt` + `I` , `M`

3. Make changes as desired.

4. Click outside comment bubble .... `Esc`

DELETE COMMENT

1. Click cell containing comment.

2. Click **Edit**, **Clear** .... `Alt`+`E`, `E`

3. Click **Comments** .... `O`

Protect Data

Prevents changes to data in cells and/or to objects (such as graphics) on a sheet. First, protect all cells and/or objects on a sheet. Then, you can unprotect specific cells or objects on a sheet that you want to be able to edit. You cannot edit, move, replace, or delete protected objects or data in protected cells.

PROTECT ALL CELLS AND/OR OBJECTS ON SHEET

1. Right-click sheet tab containing
   data to protect.

2. Click **Sheet Properties** .... `S`

3. Click [Protection] .... `Ctrl`+`Tab`

4. Select **Enable Cell Locking** .... `C`
   check box, if desired.

5. Select **Enable Object Locking** .... `O`
   check box, if desired.

6. Click [OK] .... `↵`

   NOTE: *To unprotect cells or objects, follow the*
               *same steps to deselect **Enable Cell***
               ***Locking** or **Enable Object Locking**.*

Quattro Pro 161

Unprotect Specific Cells and/or Objects

1. Select cell(s)/object(s) to unprotect.
2. Click **Fo_r_mat, Se_l_ection** .... `Alt`+`R`, `E`
3. Click `Constraints` .... `Ctrl`+`Tab`
   if necessary.
4. Select **Unprotect** radio button .... `U`
5. Click `OK` .... `↵`

FORMAT

Apply Borders

1. Select cell(s) to format.
2. Click **Line Drawing** `⊡ ▾` arrow.
3. Click border type to apply.

Align Text

1. Select cell(s) to format.
2. Click **Fo_r_mat, Se_l_ection** .... `Alt`+`R`, `E`
3. Click `Alignment` if necessary .... `Ctrl`+`Tab`
4. Set desired **Horizontal Alignment** and/or
   Vertical Alignment options.
5. Click `OK` .... `↵`

Text Alignment Shortcut Keys

To:	Press:
Center	`Ctrl`+`E`
Left-align	`Ctrl`+`L`
Right-align	`Ctrl`+`R`

Apply Font Attributes

1. Select cell(s) to format.

2. Click **Format**, **Selection** .... `Alt`+`R`,`E`

3. Click `Cell Font` if necessary .... `Ctrl`+`Tab`

4. Select desired **Font face**, **Font size**, **Text Color**, **Appearance**, and/or **Accounting style** options.

Example of selected font and attributes appears at the bottom right corner of the dialog box.

5. Click `OK` .... `⏎`

FONT ATTRIBUTE SHORTCUT KEYS

To:	Press:
Bold	`Ctrl`+`B`
Italic	`Ctrl`+`I`
Underline	`Ctrl`+`U`

Rotate Text

1. Select cell(s) to format.

2. Click **Format**, **Selection** .... `Alt`+`R`,`E`

3. Click `Alignment` .... `Ctrl`+`Tab`
   if necessary.

4. Select **Rotated** radio button .... `O`

5. Type or select degrees of rotation ..... `Tab`,`↑``↓`

   NOTE: The preview box at the bottom of the dialog box shows an example of the selected degrees of rotation.

.6. Click `OK` .... `⏎`

Wrap Text in Cells

1. Select cell(s) to format.

2. Click **Fo_r_mat, S_e_lection** .... `Alt`+`R`, `E`

3. Click `Alignment` .... `Ctrl`+`Tab`
   if necessary.

4. Select **_W_rap Text** check box........................... `W`

5. Click `OK` .... `↵`

Row height adjusts to show all text.

Format Numbers/Dates

1. Select cell(s) to format.

   NOTE: Cells can contain data or be blank.

2. Click **Fo_r_mat, S_e_lection** .... `Alt`+`R`, `E`

3. Click `Numeric Format` .... `Ctrl`+`Tab`
   if necessary.

4. Select desired format to apply.

   *NOTE: When you select a format, in most cases,
   additional options will appear in the dialog
   box for you to add more information to
   apply to the selected format.*

5. Enter any additional options if necessary.

6. Click `OK` .... `↵`

Set Default Date/Time Format

By default, Quattro Pro uses the Windows international short date format, set in the Windows Control Panel.

1. Click **T**ools, **S**ettings .... `Alt`+`T`,`E`

2. Click `International` ...., `Ctrl`+`Tab`
   if necessary.

3. Select **D**ate Format radio button .... `D`

   OR

   Select **T**ime Format radio button .... `T`

4. Select **W**indows Default radio button, or select desired date/time format at right side of dialog box.

5. Click `OK` .... `↵`

Change Text Color

1. Select cell(s) containing data to format.

2. Click **Text Color** arrow.

3. Click color to apply.

Center Title Across Cells

1. Type title in row cell .... *title*

2. Select cells in row in which you will center title.

   NOTE: *Include the cell containing the title in the selection. The title will be centered in the block of cells that you select.*

3. Click **Join and Center Cells**

Combines selected cells and centers title.

Copy Formatting

Copies cell formatting, such as boldface, font, borders, number format, text rotation, and other formats.

1. Click **QuickFormat** ![QuickFormat icon]

2. Click cell containing formatting to copy.

3. Click cell(s) to format.

4. Click **QuickFormat** ![QuickFormat icon]

Clear Formatting

Removes cell formatting, such as boldface, font, borders, number format, and text rotation.

1. Select cell(s) containing formatting to remove.

2. Click **Edit, Clear** .... Alt + E , E

3. Click **Formats** .... F

Style

SET/CHANGE NORMAL STYLE

Normal *style is the default style for data that you enter in cells. Change Normal style to change, for example, the default font or the number format.*

1. Click **Format, Styles** .... Alt + R , S

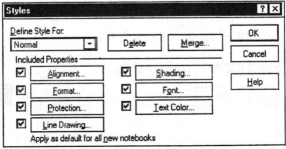

STYLES DIALOG BOX

continued...

SET/CHANGE NORMAL STYLE (CONTINUED)

2. Select **Normal** style in.............................. `↑` `↓`
   Define Style For drop-down
   list box, if necessary.

3. Set formatting options as desired.

4. Select **Apply as default for** .... `Alt`+`N`
   all new notebooks, if desired.

5. Click `OK` ....`↵`

CREATE/EDIT STYLE

1. Click **Format**, **Styles** .... `Alt`+`R`,`S`

2. Type new style name............................ *style name*
   in **Define Style For**
   text box to create style.

   OR

   Select style to edit................................... `↑` `↓`
   in **Define Style For**
   drop-down list box.

   *NOTE: If a property is included in a given style,
   the check mark to the left of the property
   is selected.*

3. Set formatting options as desired.

4. Select desired property style.

5. Click `OK` ....`↵`

APPLY STYLE FORMATTING TO CELLS

1. Select cell(s) to format.

2. Click **Style List** `Normal ▼` arrow on Property Bar.

3. Click style to apply.

DELETE STYLE

1. Click **Format, Styles** .... `Alt`+`R`, `S`

2. Select style to delete in .... `↑` `↓`
   Define Style For drop-down list.

3. Click `Delete` .... `Alt`+`E`

   NOTE: You cannot delete the Normal (default)
   style.

Apply SpeedFormat

A SpeedFormat applies many formatting attributes—such as boldfacing and a larger point size for titles or borders—to quickly format an attractive table.

1. Select cell(s) to format.

2. Click **Format, SpeedFormat** .... `Alt`+`R`, `F`

3. Select SpeedFormat from **Formats** list ...... `↑` `↓`

*The **Example** Window in the **SpeedFormat** dialog box shows the selected SpeedFormat.*

4. Deselect any check box attributes that you do not want to **Include**.

*The **Example** SpeedFormat window updates to show your selections.*

5. Click `OK` .... `↵`

Row Height and Column Width

CHANGE ROW HEIGHT

1. Select rows(s) to resize.

2. Drag top or bottom row heading border
   to desired position.

   Pointer changes to: ↕

   OR

   a. Click **Fo_r_mat**, **S_e_lection** .... `Alt`+`R`,`E`

   b. Click `Row/Column` .... `Ctrl`+`Tab`
      if necessary.

   c. Select **Set height** radio button .... `G`

   d. Type desired row height.............. `Tab`*,number*
      in **Set Height** dialog box.

   e. Click `OK` .... `↵`

CHANGE COLUMN WIDTH

1. Select column(s) to resize.

2. Drag left or right column heading border
   to desired position.

   Pointer changes to: ↔

   OR

   a. Click **Fo_r_mat**, **S_e_lection** .... `Alt`+`R`,`E`

   b. Click `Row/Column` .... `Ctrl`+`Tab`
      if necessary.

continued...

CHANGE COLUMN WIDTH (CONTINUED)

c. Select **Set width** radio button....................... $\boxed{\text{S}}$
    if necessary.

d. Type desired column width .... $\boxed{\text{Tab}}$,*number*
    in **Set width** text box.

e. Click $\boxed{\quad \text{OK} \quad}$ .... $\boxed{\text{↵}}$

SET DEFAULT COLUMN WIDTH FOR SHEET

1. Right-click sheet tab.

2. Click **Sheet Properties**.............................. $\boxed{\text{S}}$

3. Click $\boxed{\quad \text{Default Width} \quad}$ .... $\boxed{\text{Ctrl}}$ + $\boxed{\text{Tab}}$
    if necessary.

4. Type desired **Column Width**....................... *number*

5. Select desired **Unit** of measure radio button option.

6. Click $\boxed{\quad \text{OK} \quad}$ .... $\boxed{\text{↵}}$

Rename Sheet

1. Right-click sheet tab to rename.

2. Click **Sheet Properties**.............................. $\boxed{\text{S}}$

3. Click $\boxed{\quad \text{Name} \quad}$ .... $\boxed{\text{Ctrl}}$ + $\boxed{\text{Tab}}$
    if necessary.

4. Type desired **Sheet Name**.................... *sheet name*

5. Click $\boxed{\quad \text{OK} \quad}$ .... $\boxed{\text{↵}}$

The new sheet name appears on the selected sheet tab.

GRAPHICS

Charts

FLOATING CHARTS AND THE CHART WINDOW

A **floating chart** is an object on a sheet. Create a floating chart when you want to display and print the chart on a sheet.

Create a chart in the **chart window** when you want to use the chart as a slide in a slide show, or when you want to print it separately from the notebook.

You can open a chart window to edit both floating charts and charts that you created in the chart window.

The notebook contains the data for the chart. When you change the data in the notebook, charts are automatically updated.

CREATE FLOATING CHART USING QUICKCHART

Creates a floating chart on the current sheet using default chart settings. You can edit the chart.

1. Select data to chart.

   NOTE: Include any cells containing text, such as axis labels, if the text is in cells next to the data.

2. Click **Floating Chart** 📊

Pointer changes to: 📊

3. Drag on sheet to chart size.

When you release the mouse button, Quattro Pro creates the chart in the area that you defined when you dragged in step 3.

CREATE CHART USING CHART EXPERT

Starts the Chart Expert which displays a series of prompts to help you create a custom chart. You can create a floating chart or a chart in the chart window.

1. Select data to chart.

   > *NOTE: Include any cells containing text, such as axis labels, if the text is in cells next to the data.*

2. Click <u>I</u>nsert, C<u>h</u>art .... `Alt`+`I`,`H`

3. Follow Chart Expert prompts to create chart.

   To get additional help in a particular step:

   Click `Tip` .... `Alt`+`T`

   To create floating chart:

   Select <u>C</u>urrent Sheet radio button.......... `Alt`+`C`
   at Step 5 of Chart Expert prompts.

   To create chart in chart window:

   Select Chart <u>W</u>indow radio button .... `Alt`+`W`
   at Step 5 of Chart Expert prompts.

CLOSE CHART WINDOW

Click window ☒ to return to notebook .... `Ctrl`+`F4`

> *NOTE: The chart is not saved until you save the notebook (**Ctrl+S**).*

SHOW/HIDE CHART AND DRAWING TOOLS

Use for editing a floating chart in the notebook window. In the chart window, tools are automatically displayed.

Edit Floating Chart on Sheet

Display Chart Menu on Menu Bar

Click chart to add the **Chart** menu to the menu bar.

Show/Hide Chart and Drawing Tools

1. Right-click toolbar area at top of window.

2. Select/deselect **Chart** ....⌷Ⓒ⌷,⌷↵⌷
   and Drawing Tools.

Edit Chart in Chart Window

Opens a chart that you created in the chart window. You can open a floating chart for editing in the chart window. When you close the window, the floating chart is updated on the sheet.

1. Right-click any blank cell on sheet.

2. Click **Edit Chart** .... Ⓔ

3. Click chart to edit .... ↑ ↓

4. Click ⌷ OK ⌷ .... ↵

5. Edit chart as desired.

   To switch between chart window/notebook:

   a. Click **Window** .... Alt + Ⓦ

   b. Type or select window number to go to.

6. Click window ⊠ .... Ctrl + F4
   to close chart window and return to notebook.

Change Chart Type

1. Right-click anywhere on chart.

2. Click **Type/Layout** .... Ⓣ, ↵

continued...

3. Click desired chart **C**ategory .... `Alt`+`C`

4. Click desired chart type example.

5. Click `OK` .... `↵`

CHANGE TITLES AND/OR AXIS LABEL TEXT

1. Right-click title.

   NOTE: If you did not add a title to the chart
   when you created it and wish to add
   one, right-click the chart.

2. Click **Titles** .... `T`,`T`,`↵`

3. Type new/replacement **M**ain Title, **S**ubtitle,
   X-Axis Title, Y**1**-Axis Title, and/or Y**2**-Axis
   Title, as desired.

4. Click `OK` .... `↵`

MOVE CHART TITLE

In chart window, drag title to new position.

FORMAT CHART TITLE

Changes font, color, and alignment. Adds a border around
a title, and adds other formatting.

1. Click chart title to select text box.

2. Right-click title.

3. Click **Chart Title Properties** .... `C`

4. Set options as desired.

5. Click `OK` .... `↵`

CHANGE CHART DATA

1. Right-click series.

2. Click **Series** .... ⟨S⟩

   To plot different series:

   a. Click series to change (**X-Axis**, **Legend**, or a data series).

   b. Type or select cells in notebook containing data to plot.

   NOTE: *To plot the same cells but change the chart data, edit the underlying data for the chart in the notebook. When you change data in plotted cells, charts are automatically updated.*

   To add new series:

   a. Click in series after which to add new series.

   b. Click ⟨Add⟩ .... ⟨Alt⟩+⟨A⟩

   c. Type or select cells to plot.

   To remove series:

   a. Click in series to delete.

   b. Click ⟨Delete⟩ .... ⟨Alt⟩+⟨D⟩

   To reverse plot order:

   Select **Reverse Series** check box .... ⟨Alt⟩+⟨R⟩

   To reverse the orientation of a series:

   Select **Row/Column Swap** check box ..... ⟨Alt⟩+⟨C⟩

3. Click ⟨OK⟩ .... ⟨↵⟩

FORMAT CHART BORDER FOR FLOATING CHART ON SHEET

Removes or changes the border when editing a floating chart directly on the sheet (not in a chart window).

1. Right-click chart background.

2. Click **Chart Properties**.

   To remove border or change line style:

   a. Click [Box Type] .... `Ctrl`+`Tab`
      if necessary.

   b. Click desired **Box Type** line width.

   *NOTE: To remove border, click **None**.*

   c. Select **Drop Shadow** check box.................. `D`
      to add shadow behind box for
      3-D effect, if desired.

   d. Select **Transparent** check box..................... `R`
      to show cells through the chart, if desired.

   To change border color:

   a. Click [Border Color] .... `Ctrl`+`Tab`
      if necessary.

   b. Click arrow next to color drop-down
      list to open color palette.

   c. Click desired color to apply.

3. Click [OK] .... `↵`

FORMAT CHART BORDER IN CHART WINDOW

Removes or changes the border when editing in the chart window.

1. Right-click chart background.

2. Click **Background Properties** .... `B`

continued...

FORMAT CHART BORDER IN CHART WINDOW (CONTINUED)

3. Click **Box Settings** tab............................ `Ctrl`+`Tab`
   if necessary.

4. Select from **Fill Color** palette .... `↑` `↓` , `↵`
   to apply border color.

5. Click desired border type button to apply.

6. Click ⬚ OK ⬚ .... `↵`

FORMAT CHART LEGEND

*Sets font, color, borders, legend position, and other
formatting options.*

1. Click **Chart**, **Legend** .... `Alt`+`C`, `L`

2. Set options as desired.

3. Click ⬚ OK ⬚ .... `↵`

COPY CHART FORMATTING

1. Click chart to select floating chart in
   sheet or chart icon in Objects sheet.

   OR

   Click **Edit**, **Select All** .... `Alt`+`E`, `L`
   to select chart in chart window.

2. Click **Edit**, **Copy**.................................... `Ctrl`+`C`

3. Select chart to format using copied formats.

4. Click **Edit**, **Paste Special** .... `Alt`+`E`, `S`

continued...

COPY CHART FORMATTING (CONTINUED)

Paste Special Chart	? X
☑ S̲tyle	OK
☑ P̲ositions	Cancel
☑ T̲itles	
☑ D̲ata Series	Help
☑ B̲ackground	
☑ C̲olor Scheme	
☑ A̲nnotations	

PASTE SPECIAL CHART DIALOG BOX

5. Deselect **D̲ata Series** check box .... `Alt`+`D`
   so that you will not copy the data
   in addition to the formatting.

6. Deselect any other check box formats that
   you do not wish to apply.

7. Click ` OK ` .... `↵`

NAME CHART

By default, Quattro Pro names each chart Chart1, Chart2, etc.

1. Click **Objects sheet** `>|` .... `Alt`+`V`, `O`
   to go to Objects sheet.

   *NOTE: Each chart in the notebook is represented by an
            icon on the Objects sheet. The icon is located to
            the left of the first sheet tab in the notebook.*

2. Right-click icon of chart to rename.

3. Click **Icon Properties** .... `I`

4. Type new chart name ....*chart name*

5. Click ` OK ` .... `↵`

6. Click **Objects sheet** `|<` .... `Alt`+`V`, `D`
   to return to original sheet.

DELETE CHART

1. Click **Objects sheet** ⊳⎮.....................<kbd>Alt</kbd>+<kbd>V</kbd>,<kbd>O</kbd>
   to go to Objects sheet.

2. Click icon of chart to delete.

3. Press **Delete**...<kbd>Delete</kbd>

4. Click **Objects sheet** ⎮◁.....................<kbd>Alt</kbd>+<kbd>V</kbd>,<kbd>D</kbd>
   to return to original sheet.

PRINT FLOATING CHART

*Follow **Print File** procedure, page 192. Print the sheet
containing the chart as you would any other sheet.*

PRINT CHART CREATED IN CHART WINDOW

1. Click **Objects sheet** ⊳⎮.....................<kbd>Alt</kbd>+<kbd>V</kbd>,<kbd>O</kbd>
   to go to Objects sheet.

   *NOTE: The icon is located to the left of the first
   sheet tab in the notebook.*

   To select chart(s) to print:

   - **One Chart**   Click chart icon.

   - **Multiple charts**   Press **Shift** and click
                            each icon.

   - **All charts   Click **Edit**, Se**l**ect All.
     and objects**

2. Click **File**, **Print**...................................<kbd>Ctrl</kbd>+<kbd>P</kbd>

3. Set options as desired.

4. Click ⎮ Print ⎮...<kbd>↵</kbd>

Chart Slide Shows

CREATE CHART SLIDE SHOW

1. Click **Objects sheet** ⊡................... Alt + V , O
   to go to Objects sheet.

2. Click **Tools, New Slide Show**.......... Alt + T , W

3. Type **Slide Show Name** ....*name*

4. Click ⌷ OK ⌷... ↵

Light Table window for slide show appears.

OPEN EXISTING SLIDE SHOW

1. Click **Objects sheet** ⊡................... Alt + V , O
   to go to Objects sheet.

2. Double-click slide show icon.

ADD CHART TO SLIDE SHOW

1. Click **Slides, New Slide** .... Alt + S , S
   in Light Table window.

2. Click **From Existing Chart** .... E

3. Click chart to insert.................................. ↑ ↓

4. Click ⌷ OK ⌷... ↵

MASTER SLIDE

The master slide determines the default formatting, such as the background, for all slides. The master slide is optional and is the first slide in the presentation.

CREATE MASTER SLIDE

1. Click **S**lides, **N**ew Master Slide ...... `Alt`+`S`, `N`
   in Light Table window.

2. Type title information and otherwise
   format master slide.

3. Click window ☒ to close slide .... `Ctrl`+`F4`
   and return to Light Table window.

USE EXISTING CHART AS MASTER SLIDE

1. Right-click master slide in Light Table window.

2. Click **Slide Properties** .... `S`

3. Click [Master Slide] .... `Ctrl`+`Tab`
   if necessary.

4. Type chart to be on the master slide.

5. Click [OK] .... `↵`

SELECT TEMPLATE STYLE

1. Click **S**lides .... `Alt`+`S`
   in Light Table window.

2. Click **M**aster Slide Gallery .... `M`

3. Click desired template **St**yle to use.

4. Click [OK] .... `↵`

SUPPRESS MASTER SLIDE FOR INDIVIDUAL SLIDE

Prevents master slide elements from appearing in a selected slide.

1. Right-click slide to remove master from Light Table window.

2. Click **Slide Properties**...................................... `S`

3. Click ` Slide Effect ` .... `Ctrl`+`Tab`
   if necessary.

4. Deselect **Use Master Slide** check box.............. `U`

5. Click ` OK ` .... `↵`

TRANSITION EFFECTS

Sets special effects that will run when a new slide appears on the screen during a slide show. The default transition effect applies to all slides except for slides where you set the transition effect for an individual slide.

SET DEFAULT TRANSITION EFFECT FOR ALL SLIDES

1. Right-click Light Table window background.

2. Click **Light Table Properties**........................... `L`

3. Click ` Default Effect ` .... `Ctrl`+`Tab`
   if necessary.

4. Set default visual **Transition** .... `Alt`+`T`, `↑` `↓`
   Effect.

5. Click ` OK ` .... `↵`

SET TRANSITION EFFECT FOR INDIVIDUAL SLIDE

1. Click to select slide in Light Table window.

2. Click **Slides**, **Transition Effect** .... `Alt`+`S`, `T`

3. Select desired **Transition** .... `Alt`+`T`, `↑` `↓`
   Effect.

4. Click ` OK ` .... `↵`

DISPLAY TIME

Defines the number of seconds that each slide will appear before automatically displaying the next slide. The default display time applies to all slides—except for individual slides where you set a different display time.

SET DEFAULT DISPLAY TIME FOR ALL SLIDES

1. Right–click Light Table window background.

2. Click **Light Table Properties** .... `L`

3. Click ` Default Effect ` .... `Ctrl`+`Tab`
   if necessary.

4. Type or select **Display Time** .... `D`, *number*
   in **Seconds**.

5. Click ` OK ` .... `↵`

SET DISPLAY TIME FOR INDIVIDUAL SLIDE

1. Right-click (non-master) slide in Light Table window.

2. Click **Slide Properties** .... `S`

3. Click ` Slide Effect ` .... `Ctrl`+`Tab`
   if necessary.

4. Type or select **Display Time** .... `D`, *number*
   in **Seconds**.

5. Click ` OK ` .... `↵`

HIDE SLIDE

The slide will not appear in the slide show.

1. Right-click slide to hide in Light Table window.

2. Click **Slide Properties**.................................... `S`

3. Click `Slide Effect` .... `Ctrl`+`Tab`
    if necessary.

4. Select **Skip Slide in Presentation** check box... `K`

5. Click `OK`... `↵`

DELETE SLIDE

1. Click slide to delete in Light Table window.

2. Click **Slides**, **Delete Slide**............... `Alt`+`S`,`D`

MOVE SLIDE

Drag slide to new position in Light Table window.

VIEW SLIDE IN FULL SCREEN

1. In Light Table window, click slide to view in
    Full Screen view.

2. Click **Slides**, **View Slide** .... `Alt`+`S`,`V`

3. Press **Esc**... `Esc`
    to return to Light Table window.

SET SIZE OF SLIDES IN LIGHT TABLE WINDOW

1. Click **View**.. `Alt`+`V`

2. Click desired size option .... `↑` `↓`,`↵`

RUN SLIDE SHOW

Click **Slides**, **Play Slide Show** .... Alt + S , L
in Light Table window.

OR

1. Click **Tools**, **Slide Show** .... Alt + T , L , L
   Play in notebook.

2. Select slide show to run .... ↑ ↓

3. Click ` OK ` .... ↵

SLIDE SHOW SHORTCUTS

- **Go to next slide** *click left mouse button.*

- **Go to previous slide** *click right mouse button.*

- **Go to any slide** F5

- **Cancel show** .... Esc

Pictures

*To insert pictures, such as clip art and pictures on disk and
to draw pictures using drawing tools, see GRAPHICS in
WordPerfect section, page 40.*

MACRO

Record Quattro Pro Macro

*Records a macro and stores macro commands in a block of
cells that you specify. You cannot pause a Quattro Pro macro.*

1. Click **Tools**, **Macro** .... Alt + T , M

2. Click **Record** .... R

continued...

RECORD QUATTRO PRO MACRO (CONTINUED)

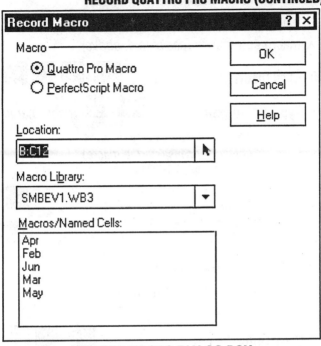

RECORD MACRO DIALOG BOX

3. Select **Quattro Pro Macro** .... `Alt`+`Q`
   radio button, if necessary.

4. Type or select first cell of block............*cell address*
   to hold macro commands in
   Location text box.

5. Click `OK` .... `↵`

6. Perform tasks to record.

7. Click **Tools**, **Macro**, **Record** .... `Alt`+`T`, `M`, `R`
   to end Record mode when finished.

8. Select first cell of block where macro
   is stored (*see step 4, above*).

continued…

RECORD QUATTRO PRO MACRO (CONTINUED)

9. Select first cell of block of cells containing macro commands (*see step 4, above*).

10. Click **I**nsert, **N**ame, **C**ells........ `Alt`+`I`,`N`,`C`

11. Type macro **N**ame .... `Alt`+`N`, *macro name*

   NOTE: *To run the macro every time the notebook opens (startup macro), name it _NBSTARTMACRO.*

12. Click `Add` .... `↵`

13. Click `Close` .... `Esc`

Record PerfectScript Macro

Records a macro and stores macro commands in a separate file.

1. Click **T**ools, **M**acro......................... `Alt`+`T`,`M`

2. Click **R**ecord .... `R`

3. Select **P**erfectScript Macro.................... `Alt`+`P` radio button.

4. Type name of file to store macro.......*filename.wcm*

5. Click `OK` .... `↵`

6. Perform tasks to record.

   To pause/resume macro:

   Click **T**ools, **M**acro, Pa**u**se...... `Alt`+`T`,`M`,`U`

7. Click **T**ools, **M**acro, **R**ecord .... `Alt`+`T`,`M`,`R` to end Record mode when finished.

Play Quattro Pro Macro

1. Click **T**ools, **M**acro .... `Alt`+`T`, `M`

2. Click **P**lay .... `P`

3. Select **Q**uattro Pro Macro radio button .... `Alt`+`Q`

4. Select macro name .... `Alt`+`M`, `↑` `↓`

5. Click `OK` .... `↵`

Play PerfectScript Macro

1. Click **T**ools, **M**acro .... `Alt`+`T`, `M`

2. Click **P**lay .... `P`

3. Select **P**erfectScript Macro radio button .... `Alt`+`P`

4. Type or select desired macro **F**ilename .... *name*

5. Click `OK` .... `↵`

Create QuickButton to Run Macro Commands

1. Create macro.(See *Record Quattro Pro Macro, page 184.*)

2. Copy commands to run when button is clicked:

   a. Select cells containing macro commands to run when button is clicked.

   b. Click **E**dit, **C**opy .... `Ctrl`+`C`

3. Create button:

   a. Click **I**nsert, **Q**uickButton .... `Alt`+`I`, `Q`

Pointer changes to: `┼ABC`

   b. Drag in sheet to size of button to create.

When you release the mouse button, the button is created.

continued...

CREATE QUICKBUTTON TO RUN MACRO COMMANDS (CONTINUED)

4. Attach macro commands to button:

   a. Right-click button.

   b. Click **Button Properties**..............................`B`

   c. Click `Macro` if necessary ....`Ctrl`+`Tab`

   d. Position cursor in **Enter Macro** text box, if necessary.

   e. Click **Edit**, **Paste**..............................`Ctrl`+`V`

   f. Use tabs to set button options if desired.

   NOTE: *For example, click **Label text** tab to **Enter Text** that will appear on QuickButton.*

   g. Click `OK` ....`↵`

When you click the QuickButton, the macro runs.

NOTEBOOK

Create Notebook

1. Click **File**, **New**...............................`Ctrl`+`N`

2. Click `OK` ....`↵`

   NOTE: *Name the new file when you save it.*

Open Notebook

1. Click **File**, **Open** ....`Ctrl`+`O`

2. Double-click filename to open from list of files.

   OR

   a. Type filename to open ....*filename*

   b. Click `OK` ....`↵`

   NOTE: *If the file is password protected, you will be prompted for the password.*

Open Notebook Automatically

Opens a particular notebook each time you start Quattro Pro.

1. Click **Tools**, **Settings**...................... `Alt`+`T`, `E`

2. Click [File Options] .... `Ctrl`+`Tab`
   if necessary.

3. Type/select **Autoload** .... `Alt`+`A` ,*path/filename*
   File.

   > *NOTE:* If the notebook is located in the default
   > folder, you only need to enter the name of
   > the file, not the complete pathname.

4. Click [OK] .... `⏎`

Set Default Folder

*The **default folder** is the folder that Quattro Pro displays
when you open a notebook. It is also the folder where Quattro
Pro saves notebooks unless you specify a different folder when
you save.*

1. Click **Tools**, **Settings**...................... `Alt`+`T`, `E`

2. Click [File Options] .... `Ctrl`+`Tab`
   if necessary.

3. Type/select **Default Folder**...................... *pathname*

4. Click [OK] .... `⏎`

Calculation Method

1. Click **Format**, **Notebook** .... `Alt`+`R`, `N`

2. Click [Recalc Settings] .... `Ctrl`+`Tab`
   if necessary.

continued...

CALCULATION METHOD (CONTINUED)

3. Select desired **Mode** radio button option:

   - **Automatic**   to recalculate intermittently.

   You will need to pause working while Quattro Pro recalculates if you select the above option.

   - **Background**   to recalculate as you work (default).
   - **Manual**   to recalculate only when you press **F9**.

4. Click `OK` .... `↵`

Summary Information

1. Click **File**, **Properties** .... `Alt` + `F`, `R`

2. Click `Summary` if necessary .... `Ctrl` + `Tab`

3. Enter notebook information, as desired.

4. Click `OK` .... `↵`

Save Notebook

1. Click **File**, **Save** .... `Ctrl` + `S`

   If saving new file:

   a. Type **File name** .... *filename*

   b. Select **Save in** folder .... `Alt` + `I`, `↑`, `↓`, `↵`
      to save in a different folder, if desired.

   NOTE: *The default folder is displayed. See **Set Default Folder**, page 189, if desired.*

2. Click `Save` .... `↵`

Back Up Notebooks Automatically

Creates copies of the notebook after a time interval that you specify.

1. Click **Tools**, **Settings**...................... `Alt` + `T` , `E`

2. Click `File Options` .... `Ctrl` + `Tab`
   if necessary.

3. Select **Timed document**...................... `Alt` + `M`
   backup check box.

4. Type or select number of **minutes** ... `Tab` , *number*

5. Click `OK` .... `↵`

Close Notebook

Click **File**, **Close** .... `Ctrl` + `F4`

Print Preview

1. Select cell(s) to print, if desired.

2. Click **File**, **Print Preview**................. `Alt` + `F` , `T`

3. Click 🖶 to print.

   OR

   Press **Esc** to exit Print Preview....................... `Esc`

Set Paper Size/Orientation

1. Click **File**, **Page Setup** .... `Alt` + `F` , `G`

2. Click **Paper Type** tab............................. `Ctrl` + `Tab`
   if necessary.

continued...

SET PAPER SIZE/ORIENTATION (CONTINUED)

To change paper size:

Select desired size from **Type** list.............. ⬆️ ⬇️

To change orientation:

Select **Portrait** radio button.................... `Alt`+`O`

OR

Select **Landscape** radio button .... `Alt`+`D`

3. Click [OK]... `↵`

Set Margins

1. Click **File**, **Page Setup** .... `Alt`+`F`, `G`

2. Click **Print Margins** tab .... `Ctrl`+`Tab`
   if necessary.

3. Type **Top**, **Bottom**, **Left**, and/or **Right** margin
   measurements, as desired.

4. Click [OK]... `↵`

Print File

1. Select cells to print if you wish to print
   only selected cells.

   OR

   Display sheet to print if you wish to print
   a particular sheet.

2. Click **File**, **Print**................................. `Ctrl`+`P`

continued...

Quattro Pro   193

3. Select **Current Sheet** radio button.......... `Alt`+`U`
   to print displayed sheet.

   OR

   Select **Notebook** radio button................. `Alt`+`K`
   to print entire file.

   OR

   Select **Selection** radio button...... `Alt`+`E`, *range*
   to print selected cells.

   NOTE: If you selected cells to print n step 1,
   ***Selection** is automatically selected, and*
   the print range is entered in the text box.

   To preview output:

   Click `Print Preview...`.............................. `Alt`+`W`

   *NOTE: See also **Print Preview**, page 191.*

   To print multiple copies:

   Type/select **Number**................. `Alt`+`B`, `↑` `↓`
   of copies.

4. Click `  Print  `

SAVE PRINT SETTINGS

1. Set Print and Page Setup options, as desired.

   *NOTE: To set Print options, press **Ctrl+P**. To set*
   *Page Setup options, select **File**, **Page Setup**.*

2. Click **File**, **Page Setup** .... `Alt`+`F`, `G`

3. Click `Named Settings`......... .... `Ctrl`+`Tab`
   if necessary.

continued...

SAVE PRINT SETTINGS (CONTINUED)

4. Type name for settings in **New Set** box..........*name*

5. Click ⌐Add⌐ .... `Alt`+`A`

6. Click ⌐OK⌐ .... `↵`

> NOTE: *Print settings are saved with the notebook. If you do not save the notebook, settings are not saved.*

PRINT USING SAVED PRINT SETTINGS

1. Click **File**, **Print**.................................... `Ctrl`+`P`

2. Click ⌐Page Setup...⌐ .... `Alt`+`A`

3. Click ⌐Named Settings⌐ .... `Ctrl`+`Tab`
   if necessary.

4. Click name of settings to use in **New Set** list box.

5. Click ⌐Use⌐ .... `Alt`+`U`

6. Click ⌐OK⌐ .... `↵`

7. Click ⌐Print⌐

Workspace

*A **workspace** is the arrangement of open files and windows on the screen when you save the workspace. Opening a workspace opens all files that were open when you saved.*

SAVE WORKSPACE

> NOTE: *Saving the workspace does not save changes to data. Save data using the **File**, **Save** command.*

1. Open files and arrange windows as you would like them to appear when you open the workspace.

continued...

2. Click **F**ile, Wor**k**space.................. `Alt`+`F`,`K`

3. Click **S**ave.. `S`

4. Type workspace **File name**................ *filename.wbs*

5. Click `Save` .... `↵`

Open Workspace

1. Click **F**ile, Wor**k**space.................... `Alt`+`F`,`K`

2. Click **R**estore .... `R`

3. Double-click workspace filename to open.

Import Data

Import a text file or another notebook. If importing a delimited text file, see **Parse** *on page 196 to parse imported data if necessary.*

1. Display sheet before which new sheet(s) will be inserted.

   NOTE: *Imports all sheets containing data in the source file if importing a notebook. Sheets will be inserted before current sheet.*

2. Click **I**nsert, **F**ile .... `Alt`+`I`,`F`

3. Type or select **File Name** to import .... *filename*

   NOTE: *File containing data to import must be closed.*

4. Click `OK` .... `↵`

Parse

Parses text divided by a separator such as a comma, semi-colon, or tab into separate cells. Parsing data is often required after importing a delimited text file. Parsing divides data into separate cells, removing the separator character. For example, if a comma separates each field, then the text before the comma is placed in a cell and the comma is removed.

1. Select block containing data to parse.

2. Click **T**ools, **D**ataTools .... Alt + T , D

3. Click **Q**uickColumns .... Q

   NOTE: *The **Block** option is selected under **Source**; address of selected block containing data to parse appears.*

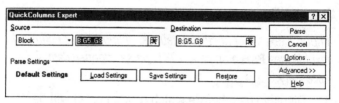

QUICKCOLUMNS EXPERT DIALOG BOX

4. Type or select **D**estination .... Alt + D ,*address* cell address, if necessary (cell in upper-left corner where parsed data will be placed).

   NOTE: *By default, the destination address is the same as the source address. If you want to overwrite data at the source, you can leave the destination address as it is.*

5. Click ⟨ **O**ptions... ⟩ .... Alt + O

continued..

PARSE (CONTINUED)

6. Select **Delimited**............... `Alt`+`D`, `↑`, `↓`, `↵`
   from **Data Type** drop-down list box, if necessary.

7. Select desired **Delimited** cell separator character.

8. Click ⌈ OK ⌉ ....`↵`

9. Click ⌈ Parse ⌉

Combine Data from Two Notebooks

1. Select cell to be upper, left-most cell of
   destination block.

2. Click **Tools**, **DataTools**................... `Alt`+`T`, `D`

3. Click **Combine Files**.................................. `B`

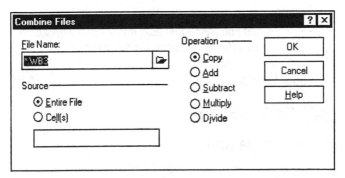

COMBINE FILES DIALOG BOX

4. Type or select **File Name** of file .... *filename*
   containing data to combine.

5. Select desired **Source** option.

   *NOTE: If you select **Cell(s)**, type cell range name
   or address in text box.*

continued...

COMBINE DATA FROM TWO NOTEBOOKS (CONTINUED)

6. Select desired **Operation** radio button option:

- **Copy** to place incoming data in destination cells, overwriting any existing data.

- **Add** to add the incoming data to the data in the destination cells.

- **Subtract** to subtract the incoming data from the data in the destination cells.

- **Multiply** to multiply the incoming data by the data in the destination cells.

- **Divide** to divide the data in the destination cells by the incoming data.

7. Select desired **Source** radio button option.

   NOTE: *If you select **Entire File**, type the filename in the **File Name** text box. If you select **Cell(s)**, type the block address in the text box.*

8. Click ⬚ OK ⬚ ....

SELECT CELLS

Select Single Cell

Click in cell.

Select Block

Drag from one corner of block to opposite corner.

OR

1. Click in one corner of block.

2. Press **Shift** and click in opposite corner.

Select Multiple BLOCKS

1. Select first block.(*Follow **Select Block** on previous page.*)

2. Press **Ctrl** and drag cells to select next block.

3. Repeat step 2, as desired.

Select Column(s)

Click column heading to select a single column.

OR

Drag across column headings to select multiple columns.

Select Row(s)

Click row heading to select a single row.

OR

Drag down row headings to select multiple rows.

Select Entire Sheet

Click in upper-left corner of row and column headings.

Pointer changes to: 🖰⇨

OR

Click **E**dit, Se**l**ect All..............................

Select Multiple Sheets

1. Click tab of first sheet to select.

2. Select first sheet.
   (*Follow **Select Entire Sheet**, above.*)

3. Press **Ctrl+Shift+PgDn**.............. Ctrl + Shift + Page Down
   to select next sheet.

4. Repeat step 3 as necessary.

Select 3-D Block

A 3-D block is the same cells in multiple sheets.

1. Select cell(s) on current sheet.

2. Press **Shift** and click tab of last sheet to include.

The cells on the current sheet are selected in all sheets up through the sheet that you selected in step 2.

Deselect

Click any cell.

Group Mode

Group mode is similar to selecting sheets. Changes to cells in any sheet are applied to corresponding cells in all grouped or selected sheets. When you select sheets, they are deselected after you make the change. In Group mode, sheets remain selected until you disable Group mode. Use Group mode to make many changes to multiple sheets without having to stop and re-select sheets each time.

1. Select sheets to group.(*Follow **Select Multiple Sheets**, page 199.*)

2. Click **V**iew, **G**roup Mode .... `Alt`+`V`,`G`

   NOTE: A thick line appears under the grouped sheet tabs.

3. To disable Group mode when finished editing and formatting sheets, repeat step 2.

DATABASE

Create Database

Create a database by having the PerfectExpert guide you through a series of prompts and dialog boxes.

1. Close any open databases if necessary.

2. Click **H**elp, Perfect**E**xpert .... `Alt` + `H` `E`

The Paradox Experts pane opens at the left side of the window.

3. Click the **Database** button in the **Paradox Experts** pane.

Displays objects you can create in Paradox.

4. Double-click ▦ [Database Expert] ... `Tab`, `↑` `↓` `↵` in list box.

5. Follow prompts to create database.

Open Database

1. Click **F**ile, **O**pen .... `Alt` + `F` `O`

2. Click **Open Table** ▦ .... `T`

3. Double-click table in database to open.

Switch to Project Viewer

The Project Viewer window shows all of the objects (such as forms, tables, and reports) in the database.

Click **Project Viewer** ▦ .... `Alt` + `T` `P`

Create Database Object Using Expert

Create objects such as queries, charts, and reports by starting an Expert that will prompt you through a series of dialog boxes to create the object.

1 Click **PerfectExpert** 🖉 .... `Alt`+`T`, `E`

2. Double-click desired Paradox Expert icon to run.

3. Make any other choices, as necessary.

Exit Paradox

Click **File**, **Exit** .... `Alt`+`F4`

EDITING DATA

Paradox stores data records in tables. You can edit data directly in the table or use a form to edit data.

Open Table

1. Double-click ▦ Tables in **Types** pane in Project Viewer window.

List of tables in current database displays in right pane.

2. Double-click desired table to open.

Open Form

1. Double-click ▤Forms in **Types** pane in Project Viewer window.

List of forms in current database displays in right pane.

2. Double-click desired form to open.

Switch to Edit Mode

Click **View**, **Edit Data** .... `F9`

     NOTE: Repeat to exit Edit mode.

Edit Part of Field (Field View)

1. **Switch to Edit Mode**, following the procedure above, if necessary.

2. Click in field to edit.

Entire field is selected.

3. Click <u>V</u>iew, <u>F</u>ield View .... `F2`

Cursor changes to I-beam. You can edit the field data.

> NOTE: *When you exit the field, you remain in Edit mode. Repeat in other fields to edit part of field. Or, press **Ctrl+F2** in step 3 and you will remain in Field View mode so that you can edit data in other fields.*

Edit Memo Field (Memo View)

1. **Switch to Edit Mode**, following the procedure on page 202, if necessary.

2. Click in memo field.

3. Click <u>V</u>iew, <u>M</u>emo View to open field ... `Shift`+`F2`

4. Type field data...*data*

5. Click <u>V</u>iew, <u>M</u>emo View to finish .... `Shift`+`F2`

Undo Last Edit

Click <u>E</u>dit, <u>U</u>ndo...................................... `Alt`+`Backspace`

OR

Press **Esc** if editing in Field view........................... `Esc`

Insert New Record

1. Position cursor in record before new record.

   > NOTE: *New record will be inserted after current record.*

2. Click <u>R</u>ecord, <u>I</u>nsert .... `Insert`

Delete Current Record

1. Position cursor in record to delete.

2. Click **R**ecord, **D**elete............................ `Ctrl` + `Delete`

Copy Data

1. Select data to copy.

2. Click **E**dit, **C**opy................................... `Ctrl` + `Insert`

3. Position cursor in destination cell.
   OR
   Select upper-left cell of destination range
   if copying a range of cells.

4. Click **E**dit, **P**aste................................. `Shift` + `Insert`

Copy Data from Same Field in Previous Record

*Enters the data that is contained in the same field as the
current field from the previous record.*

Press **Ctrl+D**... `Ctrl` + `D`

Move Data

1. Select data to move.

2. Click **E**dit, **C**u**t** .... `Shift` + `Delete`

3. Position cursor in destination cell.
   OR
   Select upper-left cell of destination range if moving
   a range of cells.

4. Click **E**dit, **P**aste................................. `Shift` + `Insert`

Insert Current Date

Press **Spacebar** three times.

> *NOTE: The current field must be a Date field.*

Paradox

Move Between Records and Fields

TO MOVE:	PRESS:
To next field (saves changes to data, if any)	`Tab` or `↵`
To previous field (saves changes to data, if any)	`Shift` + `Tab`
To field number heading in current record	`Home`
To last field in current record	`End`
To first field number heading in first record	`Ctrl` + `Home`
To last field in last record	`Ctrl` + `End`

Find Data

1. Click **R**ecord, Lo**c**ate, **V**alue .... `Ctrl` + `Z`

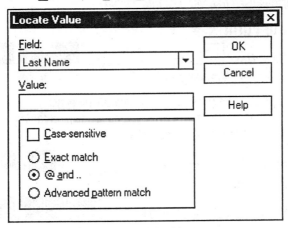

LOCATE VALUE DIALOG BOX

2. Type data ....*data*
   to find in **Value** text box.

3. Select **F**ield............... `Alt` + `F`, `F4`, `↑` `↓`, `↵`
   containing data to find.

continued...

4. Select **Case-Sensitive** check box........... Alt + C
   to find only data that matches the
   capitalization of **Value** text, if desired.

   NOTE: *For example, if you select the check box*
   option in step 4 and type jones *in the*
   Value *box, the Locate Value feature will*
   not find Jones.

5. Click OK .... ↵

Displays the next record containing data.

6. Click **Record**, **Locate Next** .... Ctrl + A
   to find next matching record.

FORMS

*A **form** is used to enter data into a table.*

Create Form

1. Click **New** .... Alt + F, N
   in Project Viewer window.

   NOTE: *The Project Viewer window displays*
   existing objects (such as forms and tables)
   in the current database.

2. Click Create New .... Ctrl + Tab
   in **New** dialog box.

3. Select **[Corel Paradox 8]** .... F4, ↑, ↓, ↵
   from drop-down list box.

4. Double-click ▦ [New Form] ...... Tab, ↑, ↓, ↵
   in list box.

5. Select method to use to create form.

   NOTE: *For help on deciding which method*
   *to use, click the **Help** button.*

Modify Form Structure
(Switch to Design Mode)

1. Double-click ▤Forms in **Types** pane
    in Project Viewer window to list forms.

2. Right-click form to change.

3. Click **Design**.. D, ↵

4. Modify forms structure as desired, following
    Work in Design Mode procedure, below.

Work in Design Mode

ADD FIELD TO FORM

1. Click **Field Palette** 🗐 in toolbar.

FIELD PALETTE

2. Select table containing fields to add from list
    at top of palette.

3. Drag field to add from Field Palette to form.

REMOVE FIELD FROM FORM

1. Click field to remove.

2. Press **Delete**.. Delete

    *NOTE: Does not remove the field from the
    underlying table.*

Draw Lines or Boxes

1. Click **Box Tool** ⬜ to draw a rectangle.

   OR

   Click **Line Tool** ▱ to draw a line.

2. Drag on form to draw lines.

Create Title/Descriptive Text

1. Click **Text Tool** 🄰

2. Drag on form.

3. Type text .... *text*

4. Follow Text Expert prompts to format text.

Preview Form with Data

1. Click **V**iew, **V**iew Data F8

2. Click **V**iew, **D**esign Form to return.................. F8

Save Changes and Exit Form Design Mode

1. Click **F**ile, **S**ave to save changes..... Alt + F , S

2 Click **F**ile, **C**lose to exit.................. Alt + F , C

TABLES

Create Table

1. Click **New** $\boxed{\square}$ .... $\boxed{\text{Alt}}$+$\boxed{\text{F}}$, $\boxed{\text{N}}$
   in Project Viewer window.

   *NOTE: The Project Viewer window displays
   existing objects (such as forms and tables)
   in the current database.*

2. Click $\boxed{\text{Create New}}$ .... $\boxed{\text{Ctrl}}$+$\boxed{\text{Tab}}$
   in **New** dialog box.

3. Select **[Corel Paradox 8]** .... $\boxed{\text{F4}}$, $\boxed{\uparrow}$ $\boxed{\downarrow}$, $\boxed{\leftarrow\!\!\lrcorner}$
   from drop-down list box.

   Displays objects you can create in Paradox.

4. Double-click ⚃ [New Table] ..... $\boxed{\text{Tab}}$, $\boxed{\uparrow}$ $\boxed{\downarrow}$, $\boxed{\leftarrow\!\!\lrcorner}$
   in list box.

5. Click $\boxed{\text{Table \underline{E}xpert}}$ .... $\boxed{\text{E}}$
   in **New Table** dialog box.

6. Select **\underline{B}usiness** radio button .... $\boxed{\text{Alt}}$+$\boxed{\text{B}}$
   to list templates for typical business solutions.

   OR

   Select **\underline{P}ersonal** radio button .... $\boxed{\text{Alt}}$+$\boxed{\text{P}}$

7. Click template closest to the type of data your
   table will contain in list of **Table templates**.

   A list of Available fields in the template appears.

8. Click $\boxed{\text{>>}}$ to add all **Available fields** from template
   to new table (**Fields \underline{i}n my table** list box).

   OR

   a. Click desired field(s) to add to table from list
      of **Available fields**.

continued…

CREATE TABLE (CONTINUED)

b. Click ⟨ > ⟩ to add selected field(s) to **Fields in my table** list box.

To remove field(s) from table:

a. Click field to remove in **Fields in my table** list box.

b. Click ⟨ < ⟩

OR

Click ⟨ << ⟩ to remove all fields.

To reorder fields:

a. Click field to move in **Fields in my table** list box.

b. Click **Change order** ⟨ ^ ⟩ to move selected field up in field list box.

OR

Click **Change order** ⟨ v ⟩ to move selected field down in field list box.

To change field name:

a. Click field to rename in **Fields in my table** list box.

b. Type desired field name.... **Alt**+**E**, *field name* in **Edit name** text box.

c. Press **Enter** .... **↵**

9. Click ⟨ Next > ⟩ .... **Alt**+**N**

10. Follow Table Expert prompts to finish creating table.

Paradox

Modify Table Structure

1. Double-click ⊞ Tables in **Types** pane in Project Viewer window to list tables.

Project Viewer window lists objects in the current database.

2. Right-click table to change.

3. Click **Res_tructure** .... T , ↵

4. Restructure table as desired, following **Work in Restructure Window** procedure, below.

Work in Restructure Window

*The **Modify Table Structure** procedure, above, must be completed prior to using any of the procedures in this section.*

ADD NEW FIELD

1. Click field before which you will insert new field.

   NOTE: New field will be inserted above the field you click.

2. Press **Insert** key .... Insert

3. Fill out new field information, as desired.

DELETE FIELD

1. Click field to delete.

2. Press **Ctrl+Del** .... Ctrl + Delete

MOVE FIELD

Drag field number heading up or down.

Password-Protect Table

1. Open **Table properties** .... `Alt`+`P`, `F4`
   drop-down list box.

2. Select **Password Security** .... `↑` `↓`, `↵`

3. Click `Define...` .... `Alt`+`D`

4. Type **Master password** .... *password*

   NOTE: *The password that you type does not*
   appear in the dialog box; asterisks (*)
   appear in the place of each character.

5. Type password again .... `Tab`, *password*
   in **Verify master password** text box.

6. Click `OK` .... `↵`

Save Changes/Close Restructure Window

Click `Save` .... `Alt`+`S`

Rename Table

1. Double-click ▦ Tables in **Types** pane in Project
   Viewer window to list tables.

2. Right-click table to rename.

3. Click **Table Rename** .... `N`

4. Type new table **File name** .... *table name*

5. Click `Rename` .... `↵`

Export Table Data to File

Creates a new file from the data in a table.

1. Click **File**, **Export** .... `Alt`+`F`, `T`

2. Type or select table containing data
   to export in **From** text box.

   NOTE: Click ⸬ *to select table.*

3. Type name of file to create ...... `Alt`+`T`, *filename*
   in **To** box.

4. Select export file format .... `Alt`+`O`, `↓` `↑`
   in **To Type** list.

5. Use active tab to select options
   for the type of file to create.

6. Click `Export` .... `Alt`+`E`

BACKGROUND

Add Background to Current Show

*Determines the available backgrounds that you can choose from when you follow the **Change Slide Background** procedure.*

1. Click **Edit**, **Background Layer**..........`Alt`+`E`, `B`

2. Click tab of background to change.

Replaces displayed background with a background you select.

   OR

   a. Click **Insert**, **New Background**....`Alt`+`I`, `N`

   b. Type desired background name ....*name*

   c. Click `OK` ....`↵`

3. Click **Format**, **Background Gallery** .....`Alt`+`R`, `B`

4. Select **Category** ....`F4`, `↑`, `↓`, `↵`
   of backgrounds to view.

5. Click desired background.

6. Click `OK` ....`↵`

7. Repeat steps 2-6 to add or replace backgrounds, if desired.

8. Click **Edit**, **Slide Layer** ....`Alt`+`E`, `Y`
   to return to slide show.

Change Slide Background for Layout

Changes the background for all slides that use a particular layout in the current slide show only.

1. Click **Edit**, **Layout Layer**.................. `Alt`+`E`, `O`

2. Click **Format** .... `Alt`+`R`

3. Click **Assign Background** .... `G`

4. Select **Layout** to change........................... `↑` `↓`

   NOTE: All slides using the selected layout will have the new background.

5. Select desired background........ `Tab`, `F4`, `↑` `↓`
   from **Available backgrounds** list.

6. Click `OK` .... `↵`

7. Click **Edit**, **Slide Layer** .... `Alt`+`E`, `Y`
   to return to your slide show.

Change Background for Current Slide

1. Click **Edit**, **Slide Layer** .... `Alt`+`E`, `Y`

2. Click **Format**, **Slide Properties** .... `Alt`+`R`, `S`

3. Click **Color** .... `C`

4. Click desired **Fill Style** in **Page Color** tab of **Page Setup** dialog box, and select options as desired.

   *NOTES: Each **Fill Style** button may show a different set of available background colors, textures, and pictures.*

   *Options depend on selected **Fill Style** button. The preview window shows a sample of the selected options.*

5. Click `OK` .... `↵`

BITMAPS

Create Bitmap

1. Click **I**nsert, **B**itmap .... `Alt`+`I`, `B`

2. Drag 🖐 to define bitmap size.

> NOTE: *Opens the bitmap editor with bitmap*
> *drawing tools at the top of the window.*

3. Create bitmap using drawing tools and menus.

4. Press **Ctrl+F4** to place bitmap................ `Ctrl`+`F4`
   on slide and return to slide show.

Edit Existing Bitmap

Opens the Bitmap Editor to edit a bitmap.

Double-click bitmap on slide.

Brush Attributes

Changes the shape and/or width of the Air Brush and Eraser
tools. Also changes the density of the air brush tool.

1. Create or double-click a bitmap.

   a. Right-click the bitmap.

   b. Click **B**rush... `B`

2. Click **Fo**r**mat**, **B**rush .... `Alt`+`R`, `B`

   OR

   Choose a **Brush** **s**hape and **B**rush width.

3. Specify the **A**ir brush density.

4. Click ⌐ OK ⌐ .... `↵`

Select Area

1. Create or double-click a bitmap.

2. Click **Edit**, **Select Area** .... `Alt` + `E`, `S`

   OR

   Click **Select Area** ⬚ on the toolbar.

3. Double-click inside bitmap frame to select entire bitmap.

   OR

   Drag inside bitmap frame to select specific area.

   To deselect area:

   Click outside selected area.

Duplicate Areas

1. Create or double-click a bitmap.

2. Select area to duplicate.

3. Hold down **Ctrl** .... `Ctrl`

4. Drag selected area to position copy.

5. Click outside highlighted area to deselect.

Move Areas

1. Create or double-click a bitmap.

2. Select area to move.

3. Drag area to new position.

4. Click outside area to deselect it.

Erase Areas

To erase selected area:

1. Create or double-click a bitmap.

2. Select area to erase.

3. Click **E**dit, **E**rase Selection .... Alt + E , E

To erase selected area:

1. Click **Erase Selection** 🖉 in toolbar.

2. Drag over area to erase.

> NOTE: To change the width of the Eraser tool,
> see **Brush Attributes**, page 216.

Make Color Transparent

Removes a color from the bitmap. You can designate only one color at a time as transparent.

1. Create or double-click a bitmap.

2. Click **Fo**r**mat** .... Alt + R

3. Click **Set Tra**n**sparent Color**............................ N

4. Select desired color from palette.

5. Click ‖ OK ‖... ↵

Special Effects

Applies special effects such as brightness, contrast, embossing, and many other effects.

1. Create or double-click a bitmap.

2. Select area to which to apply special effect, if desired.

> NOTE: To apply effect to entire bitmap, do not
> select an area.

continued...

3. Click **T**ools, Special E**ff**ects ....

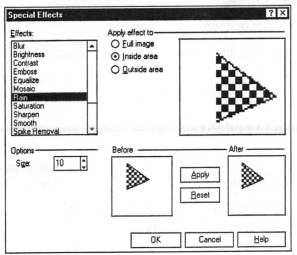

SPECIAL EFFECTS DIALOG BOX

4. Select from special **Eff**ects list box .... ⬆️⬇️

5. Select from **Options** choices, if necessary.

   *NOTE: The **Options** choices vary depending on the selected special effect.*

6. Select desired setting to **Apply effect to**.

7. If you selected the **O**utside area radio button in the step above, drag the preview rectangle on the section of bitmap image to change.

8. Click **A**pply .... Ⓐ
   to preview effect in **After** box.

9. Click [OK] .... ↵

Resize Frame/Crop Bitmap

Crops the bitmap or enlarges the area so that you can create a larger drawing.

1. Create or double-click a bitmap.

2. Drag handle $\updownarrow \longleftrightarrow \nwarrow$ to desired position(s).

   NOTE: You cannot resize the bitmap if you have rotated or skewed it.

Zoom to Edit Pixels

1. Create or double-click a bitmap.

2. Click **View**, **Zoom** .... `Shift` + `F5`

3. In **Full Bitmap** window or **Actual Size** window, click to move magnification rectangle to portion of bitmap image to edit.

4. Select desired drawing tool(s).

5. Edit pixels as desired.

6. Click **View**, **Zoom** to exit Zoom .... `Shift` + `F5`

Text Box

Wraps text to fit in text box.

1. Create or double-click a bitmap.

2. Click **Format**, **Font** .... `F9`

3. Select font and attributes as desired.

4. Click `OK`

5. Click **Text Object Tools** `A⁔` .... `Alt` + `I`, `T` on toolbar.

continued...

Presentations

6. Drag to create size to contain text.

   NOTE: The text box will expand downward as you type.

7. Type text .... *text*

8. Click outside text box to finish .... `Esc`

Exit Bitmap Editor

Click **Close** 🖉 on toolbar .... `Ctrl`+`F4`
to close Bitmap Editor and place image on slide.

OR

Click **Cancel Bitmap** ❎ on toolbar ..... `Alt`+`F`, `A`
to close without saving changes.

Convert Image

Converts bitmap image to vector image or vice versa.

1. Click **Edit**, **Slide Layer** .... `Alt`+`E`, `Y`

2. Select image to convert on slide.

3. Click **Tools** .... `Alt`+`T`

4. Click **Trace Bitmap** .... `R`
   to convert bitmap to vector image.

   OR

   Click **Convert to Bitmap** .... `V`
   to convert vector image to bitmap.

BULLETED LISTS

Create New Slide with Bulleted List

1. Click **V**iew, Slide **E**ditor .... `Alt`+`V`, `E`

2. Display slide that will precede new slide.

   NOTE: New slide will be inserted after this slide.

3. Click arrow next to **New Slide** `[⊞▾]` in status bar at bottom of window.

   *NOTE: Depending on the layout of the current slide, the **New Slide** button might display a different picture than the one shown above.*

4. Click `[⊞ Insert Bulleted List Slide]` .... `↑` `↓`, `↵`

5. Double-click bulleted list text placeholder .... *text* and type text.

   *NOTE: The placeholder displays a **Double-click to Add Text** prompt.*

6. Press **Esc** when finished .... `Esc`

Create Bulleted List on Existing Slide

Creates a new bulleted list that is not based on the master bulleted list layout. Use to place a list on an existing slide that does not have a bullet placeholder.

1. Click **V**iew, Slide **E**ditor .... `Alt`+`V`, `E`

2. Click **I**nsert, B**u**lleted List .... `Alt`+`I`, `U`

3. Click slide to insert full-page list (width of slide).

   OR

   Drag to define list area.

continued...

4. Type bulleted list text .... *text*
   pressing **Enter** to start new line, if necessary.

5. Press **Esc** when finished .... `Esc`

Edit Bulleted List

ADD NEW ITEMS TO BULLETED LIST

1. Double-click in bulleted list or placeholder.

   NOTE: *Placeholders to which you have not yet*
   *added text display a **Double-click to Add***
   ***Text** prompt.*

2. Press **Enter** to start new line, if necessary........ `↵`

   To add bulleted item at same level as current:

   Type text .... *text*

   To add bulleted item at next lower level:

   a. Press **Tab** .... `Tab`

   NOTE: *Indents to next lower level and inserts*
   bullet symbol corresponding to level.

   b. Type text .... *text*

   To add bulleted item at next higher level:

   a. Press **Shift+Tab** .... `Shift` + `Tab`

   b. Type text .... *text*

3. Click outside bulleted list to end..................... `Esc`

Change Level of Bulleted Item

1. Place cursor in bulleted line to change.

2. Press **Tab** .... `Tab`
   to move bullet down one level.

   OR

   Press **Shift+Tab** .... `Shift`+`Tab`
   to move bullet up one level.

3. Click outside list to end .... `Esc`

Delete Bulleted Item

1. Place cursor at end of line above where you
   want to delete bullet.

2. Drag to select bulleted text to delete.

   NOTE: You cannot select the bullet for the item.

3. Press **Delete** to delete selected text .... `Delete`

4. Press **Backspace** to delete .... `Backspace`
   corresponding bullet.

Format Bulleted List

*Changes the font (including colors and other attributes), the
bullet character, justification, and other format settings for each
level in a bulleted list. If formatting a master bulleted list, you
can apply changes to all master bulleted lists in the show or just
the current bulleted list. If formatting a custom list, you can
apply changes to the current list only. However, you can create a
style from your settings and apply the style to other lists.*

Change Bullet Shape

1. Right-click bulleted list.

2. Click **Bulleted List Properties** .... `E`

3. Click `Bullets` .... `Ctrl`+`Tab`

continued...

Presentations 225

4. Click level to format .... ⬆️ ⬇️

   OR

   Press **Ctrl** and click each level.............. `Ctrl`+*click*
   to format to apply same format to each.

5. Select **Bullet set** .... `Alt`+`B`, `F4`, ⬆️ ⬇️, ⮐
   to select desired bullet
   shape from different set of
   bullet symbols, if desired.

6. Select **Bullet shape** .... `Alt`+`U`, `F4`, ⬆️ ⬇️, ⮐

7. Select other bullet formatting options as desired.

8. Repeat steps 4-7 to format other levels as desired.

9. Click ⎡Apply to All⎤ .... `Alt`+`T`
   to apply changes to master bulleted lists.

   OR

   Click ⎡ OK ⎤ to apply to current list only...... ⮐

Remove Bullets

Removes bullets but leaves text in paragraphs without bullets.

1. Right-click bulleted list.

2. Click **Bulleted List Properties**......................... `E`

3. Click ⎡Bullets⎤ .... `Ctrl`+`Tab`

4. Press **Shift** button and click .... `Shift`+*click*
   to select all levels in list.

5. Select **None** in........... `Alt`+`U`, `F4`, ⬆️ ⬇️, ⮐
   Bullet shape drop-down list.

6. Click ⎡ OK ⎤ .... ⮐

CHANGE FONT AND ATTRIBUTES FOR LEVEL

1. Right-click bulleted list.

2. Click **Bulleted List Properties**.................... <kbd>E</kbd>

3. Click <kbd>Fonts</kbd> .... <kbd>Ctrl</kbd>+<kbd>Tab</kbd>
   if necessary.

4. Click level to format .... <kbd>↑</kbd> <kbd>↓</kbd>

   OR

   Press **Ctrl** and click each level to format..... <kbd>Ctrl</kbd>+*click*
   to apply same format to each.

5. Select font settings as desired.

6. Repeat steps 4 and 5 to format other
   levels as desired.

7. Click <kbd>Apply to All</kbd> .... <kbd>Alt</kbd>+<kbd>T</kbd>
   to apply changes to master bulleted lists.

   OR

   Click <kbd>OK</kbd>.. <kbd>↵</kbd>
   to apply to current list only.

APPLY BORDERS

1. Right-click bulleted list.

2. Click **Bulleted List Properties**........................ <kbd>E</kbd>

3. Click <kbd>Box</kbd> .... <kbd>Ctrl</kbd>+<kbd>Tab</kbd>

4. Select desired **Position** radio button option
   to specify where to apply borders.

5. Set desired **Frame** options to format border
   Type and **Color** as desired.

continued...

6. Click Apply to All .... Alt + T
   to apply changes to master bulleted lists.

   OR

   Click OK .... ↵
   to apply to current list only.

CREATE BULLETED LIST STYLE

Save settings in a style which you can apply to other bulleted lists.

1. Right-click bulleted list.

2. Click **Bulleted List Properties**.

3. Set formatting options as desired
   (*see procedures, above*).

4. Click Save Style .... Alt + S

5. Type style name .... *style name*

6. Click Save .... ↵

7. Click OK to close **Bulleted List Properties**
   dialog box.

APPLY BULLETED LIST STYLE

You must have created and saved a style using **Create Bulleted List Style***, above.*

1. Right-click bulleted list to format.

2. Click **Bulleted List Properties**.......................... E

3. Click Load Style .... Alt + L

4. Double-click style to apply.

5. Click OK to close **Bulleted List Properties**
   dialog box.

DRAW SHAPES

Draw Line

1. Click **E̲dit, Slide Layer** .... `Alt`+`E`,`Y`

2. Click arrow on **Line Object Tools** `/ ▾` on toolbar to open palette of line objects you can draw.

3. Click tool for shape of line to draw.

4. Click on slide to start Line mode.

5. Drag on slide to create desired line.

6. Click to end line/change line direction.

7. Double-click to finish line.

Draw Closed Shape

Draws squares, rectangles, rounded rectangles, circles, and other closed shapes.

1. Click **E̲dit, Slide Layer** .... `Alt`+`E`,`Y`

2. Click arrow on **Closed Object Tools** `□ ▾` on toolbar to open palette of shapes you can draw.

3. Click tool for shape of line to draw.

4. Drag on slide to create shape.

Draw Bezier Curves

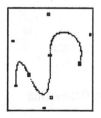

A **bezier curve** *is made up of segments of curved lines. Each* **segment** *has an* **anchor handle** *at each end.*

CREATE BEZIER CURVE

1. Click **Edit**, **Slide Layer** .... `Alt`+`E`,`Y`

2. Click **Insert**, **Shape** .... `Alt`+`I`,`P`

3. Click **Bezier** .... `Z`

4. Click crosshair pointer ‑¦‑ where you want to begin curved line.

5. Drag ‑¦‑ to desired angle of curve.

6. Click mouse button where you want the line to curve in another direction.

   NOTE: When you click, an anchor is added.

7. Repeat steps 5 and 6 as desired for each segment.

8. Double-click to finish bezier curve.

EDIT CURVE

1. Right-click anywhere on curve.

2. Click **Edit Points** .... `I`

3. Place arrowhead pointer ▶ over anchor until it changes to a crosshair pointer ‑|‑ .

   *NOTES: An **anchor** is a point where the curve changes direction.*

   Pointer changes to crosshair pointer when positioned over an anchor.

4. Click and drag to redefine curve.

5. Press **Esc** .... `Esc` to exit edit feature.

Create Shapes from Text and Graphics

QuickWarp *molds graphics into predefined shapes such as waves, pennants, crescents, and bows. You cannot, however, use QuickWarp with data charts, organization charts, or bitmaps.*

1. Select desired object or text to shape.

2. Click **Tools**, **QuickWarp** .... `Alt`+`T`,`W`

3. Select desired shape on **QuickWarp** palette.

Changes are shown in preview window.

4. Click `OK` .... `↵`

   NOTE: *To edit text that you have shaped, double-click.*

Format Shape

1. Right-click object.

2. Click **Object Properties** .... `O`

3. Set options as desired.

   NOTE: *Options vary depending on whether the object is a closed shape or a line shape.*

4. Click `OK` .... `↵`

Edit Shape

1. Select shape to edit.

   NOTE: *Property Bar tools change to graphics tools that you can use to edit the shape.*

2. Use Property Bar tools to edit shape as desired.

Copy Shape Attributes

Copies formatting such as line style, fill color, etc., from one object so that you can apply the same attributes to another object.

1. Select object with attributes to copy.

2. Click **Fo_r_mat**, **_G_et Attributes** .... `Ctrl`+`Shift`+`G`

3. Select desired radio button for attribute(s) to copy and apply.

4. Click `OK` .... `↵`

5. Select object to apply copied attributes to.

6. Click **Fo_r_mat**, **Appl_y_ Attributes** ..... `Ctrl`+`Shift`+`A`

LAYERS

Slide Layer

*Go to the **slide layer** to work with individual slides by creating and inserting graphics and text. Double-click a placeholder (for title or graphic, for example) to edit information.*

Click **_E_dit**, **Slide La_y_er** .... `Alt`+`E`, `Y`

Layout Layer

*Go to the **layout layer** to assign layouts to slides. Layouts contain placeholders for titles, charts, and other information. The actual text or graphics that appear in placeholders do not appear in the layout layer.*

Click **_E_dit**, **Lay_o_ut Layer** .... `Alt`+`E`, `O`

Background Layer

*Work with background colors, pictures, textures, patterns and fills, and the page size. Objects in the layout layer are placed on top of the **background layer**.*

Click **E**dit, **B**ackground Layer .... `Alt`+`E`, `B`

MASTER GALLERY

*A **master gallery** is a file that stores a number of different slide layouts and a consistent background design. Apply a different master to an entire presentation to change the background design of all slides in a show.*

*Use a particular layout when you create a new slide to determine which objects will appear on the slide (for example, there is a layout for a title slide and another layout for a slide containing a bulleted list). To create new slides using a particular layout, or to apply a different layout to an existing slide, see **SLIDES**, page 235.*

Apply Different Master to Current Show

Changes the design of all slides in the current show. Changes only the background layer; this feature does not affect objects on slides.

1. Click **Fo**r**mat**, **M**aster Gallery .... `Alt`+`R`, `M`
2. Select desired **Category** .... `F4`, `↑`, `↓`, `↵`
    of masters to view.

    NOTE: Select a category suitable for the type of slide show that you creating as follows:

*   **35mm**   *Use for 35mm color slides, or for color transparencies.*

*   **Printout**   *Use for black and white transparencies or black and white printouts.*

*   **Business Color, Design Nature, Theme**   *Use for slide shows that you will run on color monitors, or on the Internet.*

continued...

3. Click desired master to apply.

4. Click [Save as Default] .... `Alt`+`S`
   to set selected master as the default
   for all new presentations, if desired.

5. Click [OK] .... `↵`

Add New Layout to Master

*Open the master gallery and create a new layout. After creating
the layout, you can apply it to slides in a presentation. For
example, you might want to create a layout with placeholders
for a title placeholder, a chart, and a bulleted list.*

1. Click **File, Open** .... `Ctrl`+`O`

2. Click **File type** 🔽 to open list .... `Alt`+`Y`, `F4`

3. Click **Presentations Master (*.mst)** ..... `↑` `↓`, `↵`

4. Display master file .... `Alt`+`L`, `F4`, `↑` `↓`, `↵`
   to edit in **Look in** drop-down list box.

   *NOTES: Master gallery files are installed in the
   Corel/Suite8/Programs/Masters directory.
   This directory contains a folder for each
   master category. For example, to edit a
   master gallery in the Color category, open
   the **Color** folder.*

5. Double-click folder of master gallery to open.

6. Double-click desired master to open.

7. Click **Insert, New Layout** .... `Ctrl`+`↵`

8. Type new layout **Name** .... *name*

continued...

ADD NEW LAYOUT TO MASTER (CONTINUED)

9. Click [OK]... ⏎

10. Add placeholders, text, and/or graphics, as desired, using the **Insert** menu or the toolbar buttons.

11. Format objects that you have added.

    NOTE: *Right-click object; select **Properties** option.*

12. Click **F**ile, **S**ave..................................... [Ctrl]+[S]

13. Click **F**ile, **C**lose................................... [Ctrl]+[F4]

ORGANIZATIONAL CHARTS

Create New Organizational Chart Slide

Adds a new slide with an organizational chart placeholder.

1. Click **V**iew, **S**lide **E**ditor................... [Alt]+[V], [E]

2. Display slide that will precede new slide.

    NOTE: *New slide will be inserted after this one.*

3. Click arrow next to **New Slide** [⊡▾] in status bar at bottom of window.

    NOTE: *Depending on the layout of the current slide, the **New Slide** button might display a different picture than the one shown above.*

4. Click [⊞ Insert Org Chart Slide].............. [↑][↓], ⏎

5. Double-click chart placeholder to activate.

    NOTE: *The placeholder displays a **Double-click to Add Org Chart** prompt.*

6. Follow **Enter Organizational Chart Data** procedure, page 235.

Create Organizational Chart on Current Slide

1. Click **View**, **Slide Editor** .... `Alt` + `V`, `E`

2. Click **Insert**, **Organization Chart** ..... `Alt` + `I`, `O`

3. Click slide to insert full-page chart (width of slide).

   OR

   Drag 🖑 to define chart area.

4. Click desired chart layout to add ... `↑` `↓` `‹` `›`
   from **Layout** dialog box palette.

5. Click `OK` .... `↵`

6. Follow **Enter Organizational Chart Data**
   procedure, below.

ENTER ORGANIZATIONAL CHART DATA

1. Double-click **<Name>** or **<Title>** in `< Name > < Title >` .

2. Type text .... *text*

   *NOTE: Organizational Chart placeholders expand
   as you type, if necessary.*

3. Repeat steps 1 and 2 to fill out chart.

SLIDES

*New slides are based on **layouts** (also called **templates**).
For example, you might add a Title slide or a slide with a
placeholder for a text box. You can also insert a blank slide
that does not have any placeholders on it.*

Add Single Slide

1. Select or display slide that will precede new slide.

   NOTE: New slide(s) will be inserted after this slide.

2. Click arrow next to **New Slide** 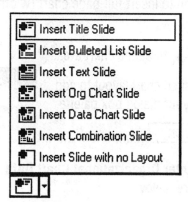 in status bar at bottom of window.

NEW SLIDE POP-UP MENU

   *NOTE: Depending on the layout of the current slide, the **New Slide** button might display a different picture than the one shown above.*

3. Click desired slide layout to insert...... ↑ ↓ , ↵

Add Multiple Slides

1. Select or display slide that will precede new slide(s).

   NOTE: New slide(s) will be inserted after current slide.

2. Click **I**nsert, **N**ew Slide .... Alt + I , N

continued...

ADD MULTIPLE SLIDES (CONTINUED)

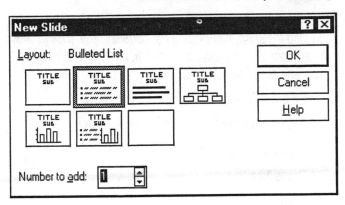

NEW SLIDE DIALOG BOX

3. Click **Layout** to apply.................... ↑ ↓ ← →

4. Type/select **Number**................. Alt + A , ↑ ↓
   (of slides) **to add**.

5. Click [OK].. ↵

Change Layout of Current Slide

1. Click **Format**, **Layout Gallery**.......... Alt + R , U

2. Select desired option .... ↑ ↓ ← →
   from **Layouts**.

   NOTE: *The preview box displays a sample of*
   the selected layout.

3. Click [OK].. ↵

Preview Slide

Plays the slide show from the current slide to the end (or you can stop the show after playing the current slide). Use to check the appearance, transition, sound, animation, and other slide show effects for the current slide.

1. Select or display first slide to preview.

2. Click **QuickPlay** at right side of window.

Starts slide show from current slide.

3. Press **Esc** to stop .... `Esc`

Print Slides

1. Click **File**, **Print** .... `Ctrl`+`P`

2. Select **Slides** radio button .... `L`

3. Type or select first slide .... `Alt`+`R`, `↑` `↓`
   to print in **Print range**.

4. Type or select last slide .... `Alt`+`T`, `↑` `↓`
   to print in **to**.

5. Click `Print` .... `↵`

SLIDE SHOW

Create Slide Show

1. Click **File**, **New** .... `Ctrl`+`Shift`+`N`

   *NOTE: [Corel Presentations 8] should be
            displayed in the top drop-down list box in
            the Create New tab of the New dialog box.*

2. Click **[Presentations Slide Show]** if necessary.

continued...

3. Click [C̲reate] .... [↵]

4. Click a master to use for the slide show.

   NOTE: *To view different masters, select from*
   ***Category** list.*

5. Click [OK] .... [↵]

Play Slide Show

1. Click **V̲iew, Play Slide Sho̲w**........... [Alt]+[V],[W]

Play Slide Show		? X
B̲eginning slide:	[Skip] 1: Welcome! ▼	P̲lay
A̲udience:	Original Slide Show ▼	C̲lose
☐	Create Q̲uickShow...	Help
☐ R̲epeat slide show until you press 'Esc'		
Highlighter co̲lor: [✎]	Width: [▬]	

PLAY SLIDE SHOW DIALOG BOX

To specify starting slide if desired:

a. Click **B̲eginning slide** [▼] .... [F4]

b. Select first slide to play .... [↑][↓],[↵]

NOTE: *Plays from the starting slide to the end of*
the show.

2. Select desired pen **Highlighter co̲lor** and **W̲idth**
   options.

   NOTE: *You can use the highlighter pen during a*
   show to emphasize text and graphics on a
   slide. Highlighting does not become a
   permanent part of the slide.

continued...

PLAY SLIDE SHOW (CONTINUED)

3. Select <u>R</u>epeat slide show .... `Alt`+`R`
    until you press 'Esc' check box option, if desired.

4. Click [<u>Play</u>] .... `↵`

RUN SLIDE SHOW

Use these features while playing a slide show.

To advance to next slide manually

Press **Spacebar**... `Space`

> *NOTE: If you have set transitions between slides,
> the next slide will automatically appear
> after the transition interval.*

To return to previous slide:

Press **Left arrow**.. `←`

To use the highlighter pen:

1. Drag mouse to highlight area on slide to
    emphasize.

2. Press **Ctrl+E** to erase highlighting.......... `Ctrl`+`E`
    if desired.

> *NOTES: Use the highlighter pen to annotate and
> otherwise mark slides during a show.
> Highlighting is not saved with slides.*
>
> *When you move to the next slide,
> highlighting is automatically erased—it is
> not saved on the slide.*

To open QuickMenu:

Right-click on slide.

> *NOTE: The QuickMenu displays options for
> volume control, going to the first slide, and
> other options for controlling playback.*

STOP SLIDE SHOW

Press **Esc** .... `Esc`

Prepare Portable Show

*Copies all files required to run the current show to disk.
Use to run a show on a computer that does not have Corel
Presentations 8 installed.*

1. Click **File**, **Show on the Go** .... `Alt`+`F`, `H`

2. Select **Repeat slide show** .... `E`
   until you press 'Esc' box, if desired.

   To change summary information, if desired:

   a. Click `Change` .... `C`

   b. Change file name and/or location
      to place your show on the Go.

   c. Click `Next >` .... `↵`

   d. Select Windows version on which
      you will be playing the show.

   e. Click `Next >` .... `↵`

   f. Select display option.

   g. Click `Finish` .... `Alt`+`F`

3. Click `Create` .... `↵`

PLAY PORTABLE SLIDE SHOW

—FROM WINDOWS DESKTOP—

1. Click `Start`

2. Click `Run...` .... `R`

3. Type path and filename of your .... *path*
   Show on the Go in **Open** text box.

   OR

   Click `Browse...` .... `Alt`+`B`
   to select path and filename of your
   Show on the Go in **Browse** dialog box.

4. Click `OK` .... `↵`

Create Custom Slide Show

Creates a show with a subset of the slides in the show. Use to show different slides to different audiences.

1. Click **View, Slide Sorter** .... `Alt`+`V`, `S`

2. Click **Tools, Custom Audiences** ...... `Alt`+`T`, `D`

3. Click `New` .... `Alt`+`N`

4. Type name for custom show ....*name*
   over **Copy of Original Slide Show**.

5. Press **Enter** .... `↵`

6. Click `OK` .... `↵`

7. Click slide to remove from current show
   to select it.

8. Click **Skip** 🔲 in Property Bar to skip
   selected slide.

continued...

9. Repeat steps 7 and 8 to remove other slides as desired.

10. Repeat steps 2-9 to create other custom shows as desired.

Save Slide Show

Click **F**ile, **S**ave .... `Ctrl`+`S`

Set Default Folders

By default, presentations that you create are stored in the MyFiles folder.

1. Click **T**ools, Sett**i**ngs...................... `Alt`+`T`, `N`

2. Double-click **F**iles .... `Alt`+`F`, `↵`

3. Click `Slide Show/Drawings` .... `Ctrl`+`Tab`
   if necessary.

4. Type/select desired **Document**................ *pathname*
   folder directory.

5. Set other default folders as desired.

6. Click `Multimedia` if desired.................. `Ctrl`+`Tab`

7. Set default folders for multimedia files as desired.

8. Click `OK` .... `↵`

Summary Information

1. Click **F**ile, **P**roperties...................... `Alt`+`F`, `R`

2. Change **Properties** dialog box................ *text*, `Tab`
   information, if desired.

3. Click `OK` .... `↵`

Copy Slide Show

1. Click **F**ile, **O**pen .... `Ctrl`+`O`

2. Type/select presentation **File** **n**ame .... *filename*
   to copy.

   To list files in different folder:

   Select desired drive .... `Alt`+`L`,`F4`,`↑`,`↓`,`↵`
   and folder from **Look in**
   drop-down list box.

3. Click Open **a**s copy .... `Alt`+`A`

4. Click **F**ile, **S**ave **A**s................................. `F3`

5. Type new **File** **n**ame .... *filename*

6. Click **S**ave .... `↵`

SLIDE VIEWS

Work in different views to perform different types of tasks.

Slide Editor View

*Use to create and edit objects on individual slides when working with the slide layer (**Edit**, **Slide Layer**).*

SWITCH TO SLIDE EDITOR VIEW

Click **V**iew, Slide **E**ditor .... `Alt`+`V`,`E`

GO TO SLIDE

Click desired slide tab at bottom of window.

OR

1. Click **E**dit, **G**o To List .... `Ctrl`+`G`

2. Click slide to go to in pop-up list.

Presentations

SHOW/HIDE RULER

Click **View**, **Ruler**.................... `Alt`+`Shift`+`F3`

ZOOM TO ANY SIZE

1. Click **View**, **Zoom**...................... `Alt`+`V`, `Z`

2. Select desired percentage radio button
    option to zoom in/out.

3. Click `OK` .... `↵`

ZOOM SPECIFIC AREA

1. Click **View**, **Zoom Area** .... `Ctrl`+`Shift`+`F5`

2. Click and drag ⊕ over area to zoom.

    To return to previous zoom:

    Click **View**, **Previous Zoom**.................... `Ctrl`+`F5`

SHOW/HIDE GRID

*Use the grid and guides in Slide Editor view for moving,
aligning, and creating objects.*

Click **View**, **Grid/Guides/Snap,** .... `Alt`+`Shift`+`F8`
Display Grid.

TURN "SNAP TO GRID" ON/OFF

Click **View, Grid/Guides/Snap,** .... `Alt`+`F8`
Snap to Grid.

> *NOTE: Even if the grid is hidden, the Snap to Grid
> feature still works.*

SHOW/HIDE GUIDES

Displays a horizontal and a vertical guide.

1. Click <u>V</u>iew, <u>G</u>rid/Guides/Snap ....`Alt`+`V`,`G`

2. Click <u>D</u>isplay Guides ....`D`

MOVE GUIDE

Drag guide vertically $\updownarrow$ and/or horizontally $\leftrightarrow$, as desired.

SET GRID/GUIDE DEFAULTS

1. Click <u>V</u>iew, <u>G</u>rid/Guides/Snap ....`Alt`+`V`,`G`

2. Click Snap <u>O</u>ptions ....`O`

3. Select options as desired.

4. Click OK ....`↵`

Slide Sorter View

Use Slide Sorter view to organize slides.

SWITCH TO SLIDE SORTER VIEW

Click <u>V</u>iew, Slide <u>S</u>orter ....`Alt`+`V`,`S`

SELECT SLIDES IN SLIDE SORTER VIEW

To select one slide:

Click slide.

To select multiple slides:

a. Click first slide.

b. Hold down **Ctrl** key...................................`Ctrl`

c. Click other slides as desired.

continued...

SELECT SLIDES IN SLIDE SORTER VIEW (CONTINUED)
To select range of slides next to each other:

a. Click first slide in range.

b. Hold down **Shift** key .... `Shift`

c. Click last slide in range.

GO TO SLIDE

1. Press **Ctrl+G** .... `Ctrl`+`G`

2. Click slide to go to in pop-up list.

COPY SLIDE(S)

Copy slide(s) and edit them to create new slide(s).

1. Click **V**iew, **S**lide **S**orter .... `Alt`+`V`, `S`

2. Select slide(s) to copy.

3. Click **E**dit, **C**opy .... `Ctrl`+`C`

4. Open another slide show in Slide Sorter view to copy slide(s) to, if desired.

5. Click slide to appear before moved slide(s).

   NOTE: The copied slide(s) will be inserted after the selected slide.

6. Click **E**dit, **P**aste .... `Ctrl`+`V`

MOVE SLIDE USING DRAG AND DROP

The slide to move and the new location should both be displayed on the screen.

1. Click **V**iew, **S**lide **S**orter .... `Alt`+`V`, `S`

2. Drag slide 🐭 to new position.

Slides are renumbered to insert the slide in the new position.

Move Slide(s)

1. Click **View**, **Slide Sorter**................. `Alt`+`V`,`S`

2. Select slide(s) to move.

3. Click **Edit**, **Cut** .... `Alt`+`E`,`T`

4. Open another slide show in Slide Sorter view to move slide(s) to, if desired.

5. Click slide to appear before moved slide(s).

   NOTE: *The moved slide(s) will be inserted after the selected slide.*

6. Click **Edit**, **Paste**............................ `Ctrl`+`V`

Delete Slide(s)

1. Click **View**, **Slide Sorter**................. `Alt`+`V`,`S`

2. Select slide(s) to delete.

3. Press **Delete** .... `Delete`

4. Click `Yes` at prompt .... `Y` to delete permanently.

Slide Outliner View

Use to work with text in the entire slide show.

Switch to Slide Outliner View

Click **View**, **Slide Outliner**..................... `Alt`+`V`,`O`

Presentations

IMPORT WORDPERFECT OUTLINE

*Creates a new slide for each first level heading in
a WordPerfect outline.*

1. Place cursor where you want outline inserted.

2. Click **Insert**, **File** .... `Alt`+`I`, `I`

3. Double-click file to insert from desired drive
   and folder(s) in **Look in** drop-down list box.

   *NOTE: You may need to select **All Files [*.*]**
   from the **File type** pop-up list box to make
   WordPerfect files visible in the **Look in**
   drop-down list box.*

*Each first-level heading in the outline becomes a slide title.
Second-level headings become subtitles. Lower-level
headings and body text are imported as bulleted items on the
slide.*

4. Edit slide text, if necessary.

EXPORT OUTLINE TO WORDPERFECT

*Creates a WordPerfect file containing your outline. Edit the
document in WordPerfect using editing and outlining features.
Then, import the outline into a show.*

1. Click **File**, **Save** to save file................... `Ctrl`+`S`

2. Click **File**, **Send To** .... `Alt`+`F`, `T`

3. Click **Corel WordPerfect** .... `W`

4. Select **Outline** radio button .... `U`

5. Click `Finish` .... `↵`

6. Edit outline text, if necessary.

ADD SLIDE IN OUTLINER VIEW

1. Click **View, Slide Outliner** .... `Alt` + `V`, `O`
2. Place cursor anywhere in slide to precede new slide.

   NOTE: New slide will follow the cursor position.

3. Press **Ctrl+Enter** .... `Ctrl` + `↵`
4. Click **Select Layout** 🔲 on Property Bar.
5. Click layout to apply........................ `↑` `↓`, `↵`
   to new slide.

ENTER/EDIT TEXT IN OUTLINER VIEW

To select text:
Drag over text to select.

To delete selected text:

Press **Delete**.. `Delete`

To demote paragraph one level:

Press **Tab** .... `Tab`

To promote paragraph one level:

Press **Shift+Tab** .... `Shift` + `Tab`

FIND TEXT

1. Click **View, Slide Outliner** .... `Alt` + `V`, `O`
2. Click **Edit, Find and Replace** .... `Ctrl` + `F`
3. Type **Find** text... *text*
4. Click `Find Next` .... `↵`
5. Repeat Step 4 as desired.
6. Click `Close` .... `Esc`
   to close **Find and Replace** dialog box when finished.

SPELL CHECK TEXT

1. Click **View**, **Slide Outliner** .... `Alt`+`V`,`O`
2. Click **Tools**, **Spell Check** .... `Ctrl`+`F1`
3. Follow prompts in **Writing Tools** dialog box, if necessary.

GRAPHICS

To use Presentation tools to create graphics, see **DRAW SHAPES**, *page 228, and* **BITMAPS**, *page 216.*

Import Graphic

1. Click **View**, **Slide Editor** .... `Alt`+`V`,`E`
2. Display slide on which to place graphic.
3. Click **Insert**, **Graphics** .... `Alt`+`I`,`G`
4. Click **From File** .... `F`
5. Double-click graphic file to import.

Insert Clipart

1. Click **Edit**, **Slide Layer** .... `Alt`+`E`,`Y`
2. Click **Insert**, **Graphics** .... `Alt`+`I`,`G`
3. Click **Clipart** .... `C`

   NOTE: When you install Corel Suite 8, not all clipart images are installed. To access all images, place the Corel CD in the drive. You can then click the **CD Clipart** *tab to browse images on the CD.*

4. Drag image from **Scrapbook** dialog box to slide.
5. Click ☒ to close Scrapbook.

Insert TextArt

*See **TEXTART**, page 128, in the WordPerfect section of this guide.*

Create Chart

1. Click **I**nsert, Ch**a**rt........................ `Alt`+`I`, `A`

2. Drag 🖱 on page to create chart placeholder.

3. Select **C**hart type to create........... `↑` `↓` `←` `→`

4. Click `OK` .... `↵`

5. Edit chart data as desired in Datasheet.

   NOTES: When the Datasheet is active, you can use the
          Data menu to edit it. You can also use
          QuickMenus to work with datasheets. Right-
          click on part of the datasheet (such as a column
          or row heading) to open a QuickMenu.

          Use the **Chart** menu and QuickMenus (right-click
          on an area of the chart) to work with charts.

6. Press **Esc** to finish .... `Esc`

SOUND CLIPS

Record Sound File

If you have an internal sound card, or an external device and a microphone, you can record a sound file which you can link to specific slides.

1. Click **I**nsert, **S**ound .... `Alt`+`I`, `S`

2. Click `Sound` .... `Ctrl`+`Tab`

3. Click `Record...` .... `Alt`+`R`

continued...

Presentations 253

4. Click **Record** `[  ●  ]`

5. Click **Stop** `[  ■  ]`

6. Click **F**ile, **S**ave .... `Alt`+`F`, `S`
   in **Sound-Sound Recorder** dialog box.

7. Type **File name** .... *filename*

8. Click `[ Save ]` .... `↵`

9. Click **Sound Recorder** dialog box ..... `Alt`+`F`, `X`
   to return to **Slide Properties** dialog box.

   To add sound file to current slide, if desired:

   Type or select sound file .... `Alt`+`W`, *filename*
   name in **W**ave text box.

10. Click `[ OK ]` .... `↵`

Add Sound Clip or Play CD

1. Click **I**nsert, **S**ound .... `Alt`+`I`, `S`

2. Click `[ Sound ]` .... `Ctrl`+`Tab`

3. Type/select **W**ave file .... *filename*

   OR

   Type or select **MI**DI file .... `Alt`+`M`, *filename*

   OR

   a. Click 🌐 next to **CD** text box.

   b. Set options as desired.

   c. Click `[ OK ]` .... `↵`

continued..

ADD SOUND CLIP OR PLAY CD (CONTINUED)

4. Deselect **Save within slide** .... `Alt`+`D`
   show document check box, if desired.

   NOTES: If you save the sound file as part of the
   slide show document, the presentation file
   size becomes larger, but the sound file will
   always be available. If you deselect this
   option, the presentation will attempt to
   locate the sound file in the specified path.

   NOTE: This feature does not apply to CD files.

5. Select **Loop sound** check box, if desired, to repeat
   playback during show.

   NOTE: Repeatedly plays until either the next
   sound file plays or the sound is manually
   stopped during the slide show.

6. Adjust volume using sound meter (**Soft** to **Loud**).

   NOTE: This feature sets the default volume. You
   can also adjust the volume during the slide
   show.

7. Click `Play Sound` to test, if desired .... `Alt`+`S`

8. Select **Apply to all slides in show** .... `Alt`+`A`
   check box to play sound when each
   slide appears on the screen.

   OR

   Click `▼` in slide drop-down list box
   (bottom, right side of dialog box) to
   select slide to add sound file to.

9. Click `OK` .... `↵`

SPEAKER NOTES

Creates speaker notes for each slide in a show. You can then print and use them as cue cards or as handouts for your audience.

Create Speaker Notes

1. Click **Fo**rmat, **S**lide Properties .... `Alt`+`R`, `S`

2. Click **Speaker N**otes .... `N`

3. Click `Speaker Notes` .... `Ctrl`+`Tab`

4. Click `▾` in slide drop-down list box (bottom, right side of dialog box) to select slide to contain speaker notes.

5. Click `Insert Text from Slide` .... `Alt`+`I` if desired.

6. Type note text .... *note*

7. Repeat steps 4-6 to add notes for more slides as desired.

8. Click `OK` .... `↵`

Print Speaker Notes

1. Click **F**ile, **P**rint .... `Ctrl`+`P`

2. Click `Print` if necessary .... `Ctrl`+`Tab`

3. Select **Sp**eaker Notes radio button .... `P`

4. Type or select **Nu**mber .... `Alt`+`M`, *number* **of slides per page** in text box.

5. Set other options as desired.

continued...

PRINT SPEAKER NOTES (CONTINUED)

To preview printed notes:

a. Click | Print Preview | .... `Alt` + `W`

b. Click **PgUp** or **PgDn** .... `Page Up` or `Page Down`
   to view pages.

c. Press **Esc** .... `Esc`
   to exit Print Preview.

6. Click | Print | .... `↵`

TEXT BOXES AND TITLES

Create New Slide with Text and Titles

1. Click **View**, **Slide Editor** .... `Alt` + `V`, `E`

2. Display slide that will precede new slide.

3. Click arrow next to **New Slide** in status bar
   at bottom of window.

   *NOTE: Depending on the layout of the current slide,
   the **New Slide** button might display a
   different picture than the one shown above.*

4. Click | Insert Text Slide | .... `↑` `↓`, `↵`

   *NOTE: Inserts a new slide with a title, subtitle, and
   text box.*

5. Double-click desired placeholder(s) .... *text*
   and type text.

6. Press **Esc** when finished .... `Esc`

Create Text Box

Create text boxes to add text that contains more than one line.

1. Click **View**, **Slide Editor** .... `Alt`+`V`,`E`

2. Display slide on which to place text box.

3. Click arrow next to **Text Object Tools** `A▾`
   on toolbar to display text object tools palette.

4. Click **Text Box** `A`

5. Drag 🖑 on slide to create text box.

   NOTE: *The text box will be as high as a single line
   and as wide as you want it to be. When
   you add text, the text box will expand to
   allow for more lines of text.*

6. Type text .... *text*

   OR

   Complete the **Import Text File into Text Box**
   procedure, below.

7. Click outside box to finish .... `Esc`

IMPORT TEXT FILE INTO TEXT BOX

1. Double-click text box.

2. Click **Insert**, **File** .... `Alt`+`I`,`I`

3. Double-click text (.txt) file to import.

RESIZE TEXT BOX

When you resize a text box, text in the box wraps to fit.

1. Click text box to select it.

2. Drag handle ⬁ ⬌ to new size.

Create Text Line for Title

Creates a text box that is only one line long. Use for titles and subtitles.

1. Click **V**iew, Slide **E**ditor .... `Alt`+`V`,`E`

2. Display slide on which to place graphic.

3. Click **I**nsert, Te**x**t Line .... `Alt`+`I`,`X`

4. Click "⊥" on far left side of slide
   (creates text line the width of the slide).

5. Type text .... *text*

6. Press **Enter** .... `↵`

Insert Current Date/Time

1. Position cursor in text box to
   contain date.

2. Click **I**nsert, **D**ate/Time .... `Alt`+`D`

3. Click format to use .... `↑` `↓`

4. Select **K**eep the inserted .... `Alt`+`K`
   date current check box, if desired.

   NOTE: *Changes the date to the current date each
   time you open or print the show.*

5. Click `Insert` .... `↵`

Insert Symbol

1. Position cursor in text box to contain symbol.

2. Click **Insert, Symbol** .... `Ctrl` + `W`

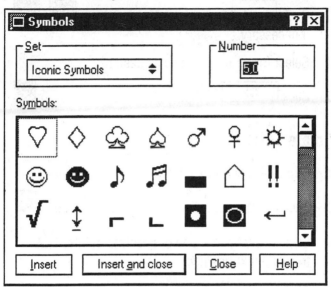

SYMBOL DIALOG BOX

3. Select from **Set** .... `Alt` + `S`, `↑` `↓`
    drop-down list box to view
    different symbols, if desired.

4. Click symbol to insert ..... `Alt` + `M`, `↑` `↓` `←` `→`

5. Click ⌐Insert and close⌐ .... `Alt` + `A`
    to insert symbol and close **Symbols** dialog box.

    OR

    a. Click ⌐Insert⌐ .... `↵`

    b. Repeat steps 3-5, as desired, to insert more
        symbols.

Change Font

1. Click text box or title to select it.

2. Click **Fo_r_mat, _F_ont** .... `F9`

3. Click `Font` .... `Ctrl`+`Tab`
    if necessary.

4. Select formatting options as desired.

5. Click `OK` .... `↵`

Rotate Text

1. Right-click text box or title.

2. Click **_R_otate** .... `R`

3. Click arrow handle, and drag rotate pointer ↻
    to rotate text box/title.

4. Click outside text box/title to finish.

Align Text

1. Click text box to select it.

2. Click **Justification** 🗒 on the Property Bar.

    *NOTE: The appearance of the toolbar **Justification**
    button changes with the option selected.
    Therefore, the button shown above may
    not be the same as on your system.*

continued…

3. Click `☰ Center` .... `Ctrl`+`E`
   to center text.

   OR

   Press `☰ Right` .... `Ctrl`+`R`
   to right align text.

   OR

   Press `☰ Left` .... `Ctrl`+`L`
   to left align text.

4. Click outside text box to finish .... `Esc`

Thesaurus

*See **THESAURUS**, page 129 in the **WordPerfect** section of this guide.*

TRANSITIONS

Sets the time interval the slide is displayed on the screen during a slide show before automatically advancing to the next slide. This feature also applies special effects to the slide and slide objects when the slide is displayed in the slide show.

Set Slide Transition Effects

1. Right-click slide background.

2. Click **Transition** .... `I`

3. Click `Transition` .... `Ctrl`+`Tab`

4. Select transition effects as desired.

continued...

SET SLIDE TRANSITION EFFECTS (CONTINUED)

5. Select **Apply to all slides**...................... `Alt`+`A`
    in slide show check box, if desired.

    OR

    Click `▶` to go to next slide to set transition
    effects, if desired.

    OR

    Click `▼` in slide pop-up list box (bottom,
    right side of dialog box) to select slide to
    set transition effects for.

*A preview of the selected transition effect appears in the
preview window in the upper-right corner of the **Transition**
tab in the **Slide Properties** dialog box.*

6. Click `OK` .... `↵`

    NOTES: *In Slide Sorter view, transition effect names
    appear under each slide.*

    *In Slide Editor view, the transition effect
    name for the current slide is displayed in the
    Slide Transition drop-down list on the
    Property Bar. You can also select a different
    transition effect in the Property Bar.*

Animate Objects

*Applies animation effects and sets the order in which objects
will appear on the slide.*

1. Click **View**, **Slide Editor** .... `Alt`+`V`, `E`

2. Display slide containing objects to animate.

3. Right-click object to animate.

4. Click **Object Animation** .... `N`

continued...

Presentations 263

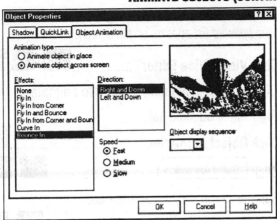

OBJECT ANIMATION TAB, OBJECT PROPERTIES DIALOG BOX

5. Select desired **Animation type** radio button setting.

6. Select from **Effects** list .... Alt + E , ↑ ↓

    NOTE: When you select an option, the preview window shows an example of the effect.

7. Select desired **Direction** .... Alt + D , ↑ ↓
    in which the object will appear.

    NOTE: Direction options vary depending on the selected animation effect.

8. Select **Speed** at which the object will appear.

9. Select an **Object display** .... Alt + O , ↑ ↓
    sequence if animating multiple objects on slide.

    NOTE: The display sequence determines the order in which each object will appear on the screen.

10. Click ⟦ OK ⟧ .... ↵

11. Repeat from step 2 to animate next object, if desired.

Animate Bulleted List

Applies special effects, such as adding one bullet at a time when the bulleted list appears on the screen.

1. Click **View, Slide Editor** .... `Alt`+`V`, `E`
2. Display slide containing objects to animate.
3. Right-click bulleted list.
4. Click **Object Animation** .... `N`
5. Click `Bullet Animation` .... `Ctrl`+`Tab`
6. Set animation options as desired.
7. Click `Apply to All` .... `Alt`+`T`
   to apply to all master bulleted lists.

   OR

   Click `OK` .... `↵`
   to apply to current bulleted list only.

Set Bulleted List/Objects Display Sequence

On slides that have both bulleted lists and objects, by default, the bulleted list is displayed first followed by the objects. Use this procedure to display objects first.

1. Right-click slide background.
2. Click **Display Sequence** .... `D`
3. Click `Display Sequence` .... `Ctrl`+`Tab`
   if necessary.
4. Select **Before the bulleted list** or **After the bulleted list** radio button option under **Animated objects are displayed** option.
5. Click `OK` .... `↵`

Set Automatic Advance to Next Slide

During slide show playback, you can either move to the next slide manually by pressing a key or you can automatically advance to the next slide after a specified number of seconds.

1. Right-click slide background.

2. Click **Display Sequence**................................. D

3. Click Display Sequence .... Ctrl + Tab
   if necessary.

4. Type/select time...................... T , Tab , *number*
   to display slide in **After
   a delay of** text box.

5. Click OK .... ↵

Assign Key to Advance to Particular Slide

1. Click **Format**, **Slide Properties** .... Alt + R , S

2. Click **QuickKeys**.................................. K

3. Click QuickKeys .... Ctrl + Tab
   if necessary.

4. Click desired key in **Keystrokes** list box .... ↑ ↓

   NOTE: *This is the key that you will press during a
   slide show to advance directly to a
   particular slide.*

5. Select slide.................... Alt + G , Tab , F4 , ↵
   to advance to from **Go to** list.

6. Repeat steps 4 and 5 as desired,
   to activate other keys.

continued…

ASSIGN KEY TO ADVANCE TO PARTICULAR SLIDE (CONTINUED)

7. Select **Apply to all slides**....................... `Alt` + `A`
   in slide show check box to have key(s)
   available when any slide is displayed.

8. Click `OK` .... `↵`

Assign Key to Play Sound

1. Click **Fo_r_mat**, **_S_lide Properties** .... `Alt` + `R`, `S`

2. Click **Quick_K_eys** .... `K`

3. Click `QuickKeys` .... `Ctrl` + `Tab`
   if necessary.

4. Click desired key in **_K_eystrokes** list box .... `↑` `↓`

   *NOTE: This is the key that you will press during a
   slide show to play the sound.*

5. Select **Play Sound** from **A_c_tion** list .... `Alt` + `C`

6. Click `Sound...` .... `Alt` + `S`

7. Type or select pathname of **_W_ave**, **_M_IDI**, or **_C_D**
   sound file to play (*see **Add Sound Clip or Play CD**
   procedure, page 253, for more information*).

8. Select **Loop sound** check box, if desired, to play
   the sound continuously until next sound.

9. Adjust volume using sound meter (**Soft** to **Loud**).

10. Click `Play Sound` .... `Alt` + `S`
    to test volume and playback, if desired.

continued...

11. Click ⬚ OK ⬚ .... ⮐

   To assign key to stop sound, if desired:

   a. Click desired key .... ↑ ↓
      in **Keystrokes** list box (*step 4, above*).

   b. Select **Stop** ... Alt + C , Tab , Tab , F4 , ↓ , ⮐
      Sound from **Action** list.

12. Click ⬚ OK ⬚ .... ⮐

Hide Slide

The slide will not appear when you play the slide show.

1. Right-click slide background.

2. Click **Display Sequence** .... D

3. Click ⬚ Display Sequence ⬚ .... Ctrl + Tab
   if necessary.

4. Select **Do not include** .... Alt + N
   this slide (skip) check box.

5. Click ⬚ OK ⬚ .... ⮐

WORK WITH OBJECTS

Work with objects such as bulleted lists, titles, placeholders, graphics, and text boxes on a slide.

Select Object(s)

If you are unable to select an object, then the object is on a different layer than the one you are working on. For example, you cannot select an object that is on the layout layer when you are working in the slide layer.

SELECT SINGLE OBJECT

Click object.

SELECT MULTIPLE OBJECTS OF SAME TYPE

Press **Ctrl** and click each object.

SELECT ALL OBJECTS OF SAME TYPE ON SLIDE

For example, selects all titles or all bulleted lists on a slide.

1. Click first object.
2. Click **E**dit, Se**l**ect, **L**ike .... `Alt`+`E`, `L`, `L`

SELECT ALL OBJECTS ON SLIDE

Click **E**dit, Se**l**ect, **A**ll .... `Ctrl`+`A`

Move Objects

MOVE OBJECT ON SAME SLIDE

Drag object to new location.

MOVE OBJECT TO A DIFFERENT SLIDE

1. Select object(s).
2. Click **E**dit, Cu**t** .... `Ctrl`+`X`
3. Display slide to move object to.
4. Click **E**dit, **P**aste .... `Ctrl`+`V`

Copy Objects

COPY OBJECT USING CLIPBOARD

1. Select object(s) to copy.
2. Click **E**dit, **C**opy .... `Ctrl`+`C`
3. Display slide on which to place copied object, if necessary.
4. Click **E**dit, **P**aste .... `Ctrl`+`V`

DUPLICATE OBJECT

1. Select object(s) to duplicate.
2. Press **Ctrl** and drag object....................`Ctrl`+*drag*
   to location in which to place copy.

Rotate Object

1. Select object to rotate.
2. Right-click.
3. Click **R**otate ....`R`
4. Click arrow handle, and drag rotate pointer ↻
   to rotate object.
5. Click outside object to finish.

Apply 3-D Effect to Graphic

You cannot edit text after you have applied 3-D effects because doing so converts the text to a graphic. You cannot apply 3-D effects to bulleted lists, bitmaps, data charts, or organization charts.

1. Select object to appear as three-dimensional.
2. Click **T**ools, **Quick3**-D ....`Alt`+`T`, `3`
3. Click `Rotation` ....`Ctrl`+`Tab`
   if necessary.
4. Select desired **R**otation option.....`↑` `↓` `←` `→`
   from palette.
5. Click `Perspective` ....`Ctrl`+`Tab`
6. Select desired **P**erspective ....`↑` `↓` `←` `→`
   option from palette.

continued…

APPLY 3-D EFFECT TO GRAPHIC (CONTINUED)

7. Set **Color adjustment**............... <kbd>Alt</kbd>+<kbd>A</kbd>, <kbd>←</kbd><kbd>→</kbd>
   using contrast meter (**Dark** to **Light**).

8. Click <kbd>OK</kbd> .... <kbd>↵</kbd>

Play Sound when Object is Clicked

Plays a sound when the object is clicked during a slide show.

1. Right-click object.

2. Click **QuickLink**... <kbd>Q</kbd>

3. Click <kbd>Sound...</kbd> .... <kbd>Alt</kbd>+<kbd>S</kbd>

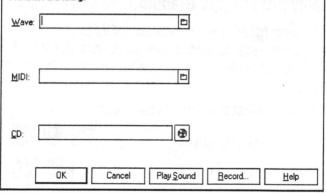

SOUND DIALOG BOX

4. Type or select **Wave**, **MIDI**, or **CD** sound file to
   play. (*See **Add Sound Clip or Play CD** procedure,
   page 253, for more information.*)

5. Select **Loop sound** check box, if desired, to play the
   sound continuously until next sound.

continued...

PLAY SOUND WHEN OBJECT IS CLICKED (CONTINUED)

6. Adjust volume using sound meter (**Soft** to **Loud**).

7. Click Play **S**ound .... **Alt**+**S**
   to test volume and playback, if desired.

8. Click OK twice .... ⏎, ⏎

Go to Another Slide when Object is Clicked

Displays a slide in the current slide show when the object is clicked during a slide show.

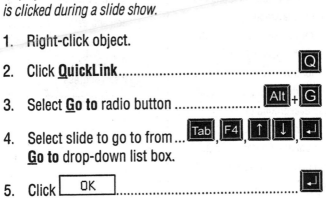

1. Right-click object.

2. Click **Q**uickLink .... **Q**

3. Select **G**o to radio button .... **Alt**+**G**

4. Select slide to go to from ... **Tab**, **F4**, ↑ ↓, ⏎
   Go to drop-down list box.

5. Click OK .... ⏎

Index

Index

275

Index

Index

Index

Index

Index

287

Index

289

Index   **291**

Index

Index

Index

VISUAL REFERENCE BASICS

Teaches 100 Basic Software Functions

Color pictures & callouts teaches the 100 basic functions of your software, explaining your computer screen—icons and dialog boxes.

Each page gives you one of the 100 basic functions of your favorite software!

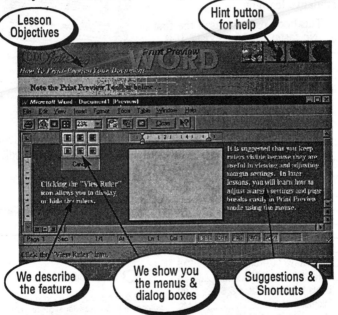

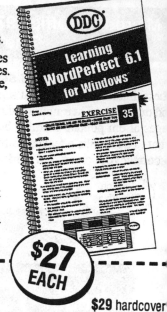

(DDC) *Short Course Learning*

pproximately 25 hours f instruction per book

We sliced our learning books o short courses, *introductory* and *intermediate*.

omplete with Lessons & Exercises

We extracted pages from our Fast-teach Learning books to create shorter versions.

Each book comes with a data disk to eliminate typing the exercise.

$25 EACH incl. book & data disk

(DDC) *Publishing*
275 Madison Avenue
NY, NY 10016

Phone (800) 528-3897
Fax (800) 528-3862

New Short Courses
(College Level) ....$25ea.

Teacher Manual and Exercise
Solutions on Diskette ....$12ea.
Files saved in Word 7

No Teacher Manual

More Quick Reference Guides

---------- ORDER FORM ----------

DDC Publishing   275 Madison Ave. NY, NY 10016 $**12**ea.

QTY.	CAT. NO.	DESCRIPTION

☐ Check enclosed. Add $2.50 for post. & handling & $1.50 post. for ea. add. guide.
NY State res. add local sales tax.

☐ Visa   ☐ Mastercard   *100% Refund Guarantee*

No._____ Exp._____

Name_____

Firm _____

Address_____

City, State, Zip _____

Phone (800)528-3897   Fax (800)528-3862
SEE OUR COMPLETE CATALOG ON THE INTERNET
http://www.ddcpub.com

8/19